AF425312

Reprints from the Royal Engineers Journal
By pagesofpages.com

Green, Miriam. *A Lady's Experiences in the Great Siege of Gibraltar (1779-83). The Journal of Miriam Green, wife of Lieut.-Colonel Green, Chief Engineer of Gibraltar.* Edited by Col. E. R. Kenyon, R. E. ii, 114 p. ISBN 979-8-9899308-0-7.

Reprinted from the Royal Engineers Journal Vols. XV and XVI, 1912.

Jones, Rice. *An Engineer Officer Under Wellington in the Peninsular. The Diary and Correspondence of Lieut. Rice Jones, R.E., During 1808-9-10-11-12.* Edited by Commander the Hon. Henry N. Shore, Late R.N. iii, 122p. ISBN 979-8-9855566-7-4. Also available as a Kindle e-book.

Reprinted from the Royal Engineers Journal Vols. XVI and XVII, 1912-13.

Thackeray, Edward T. *Sieges and the Defence of Fortified Places by the British and Indian Armies in the XIXth Century.* iii, 329p. ISBN 979-8-9855566-8-1.

Reprinted from the Royal Engineers Journal Vols. XIX to XXIII, 1914-1916.

RECOLLECTIONS OF A SEA LIFE

RECOLLECTIONS OF A SEA LIFE
BY A MIDSHIPMAN OF THE LAST CENTURY

AS PUBLISHED IN THE UNITED SERVICE JOURNAL 1831-1832

BY ROBERT CAMPBELL, COMMANDER, RN

EDITED BY GARY MENCHEN

2024
pagesofpages.com
Waterville, Maine

Contents

Introduction

The reminiscences in the following pages appeared in the *United Service Journal, and Naval and Military Magazine* in 1831 and 1832, a time when that journal was one of the most popular in Great Britain. The journal was a mixture of reminiscences such as this, historical accounts of battles, reviews, obituary notices, and writings on the various facets of military and naval science. Despite being written primarily by and for current and former officers it had a large general circulation. Many of the popular memoirs of the Napoleonic Wars first appeared on its pages; most were also published in book form, but these reminiscences were not, the author having died before completion.

The author was Robert Campbell, who began as a Midshipman in 1795, probably 14 or 15 years of age. He ended his career as a Commander, and Commandant of the naval establishment on the island of Ascension, a "stone frigate" settled in 1815 shortly after Napoleon was imprisoned at St. Helena. His tenure there was from 1819 to 1823; neither that assignment nor any possible subsequent assignment appears in the navy lists. He is reticent about his family background, but over the course of the reminiscences we learned that he was accompanied by a younger brother when he first became a midshipman, and that two older brothers had also been in the navy, and had died in the West Indies.

These memoirs are followed by two brief writings by Captain Sir Basil Hall, who had served under Campbell and become friends with him. Both area nice appreciation of him as a man and an officer, and contain some distinctive accounts of his character. The first was published in the *United Service Journal* when the death of the author of the "Reminiscences" was announced; the second was in a preface to a book written by Campbell's widow, Eliza Constantia Campbell, née Pryce: *Tales About Wales, with a Catechism of Welsh History*, second edition 1837. Her dates were 1796 to 1864; she married Campbell in 1827. They had one son, Lewis Campbell, who became a well-known classical scholar.

Portions of Campbell's early career are described in his memoirs. Basil Hall in his two notices of Campbell provides a few more details, and a few scattered issues of the Navy Lists provide still more information.

Campbell generally only identifies the first letter of the names of the ships he was on, but we know it was the HMS Active that went aground off the island of Anticosta while transporting a new Governor-General to Canada, 1796. He was on the HMS Belliqueux, a year or two later.

As of the April 1813 Steele's *Original and Correct List of the Royal Navy,* he was on the H.M.S. Minden, 74 guns, Captain Alexander Skene. On the same ship, the next year, he is listed as first lieutenant, with Joseph Prior captain. This was the flagship of Admiral Hood.

We know from Sir Basil Hall's brief accounts of Campbell that he (Hall) was lieutenant on a ship where Campbell was first lieutenant, for which the Minden fits; but we know separately that Hall first joined Admiral Hood's flagship when Hood was still on the HMS Illustrious, and that Hood transferred his flag to the Minden in 1813, so it is possible Campbell was also on the Illustrious prior to the Minden.

In 1816 he is shown on the Hesper, 18 guns, in the East Indies. By the end of 1816 he was acting Captain of the Hesper, due to the death of the previous captain. And finally, it appears he ended his career as Commandant at Ascension from 1819 to 1823. He was promoted to the rank of Commander July 12, 1821.

It is interesting to compare Campbell's accounts of his experiences as a midshipman with those of Frederick Marryat's, whose first novel, *The Naval Officer; or Scenes and Adventures in the Life of Frank Midmay* had been published in 1829, and provided a rather frank description of the experiences a young boy might encounter when joining a ship as a midshipman; Campbell perhaps hinted of this when he wrote that

> "as the First-Lieutenant did not think their [members of the midshipmen's mess] manners very exemplary, he very kindly and considerately put the other youngster and myself to mess with the gunner, a veteran seaman, from whom we heard nothing worse than some superstitious notions about foretelling the weather"

In the Journal's own "Notice of the Late Captain Robert Campbell, R.N." they wrote that he was

one possessed of excellent taste, judgment, and right feeling in
all matters, private or professional

Sir Basil Hall also wrote about his experiences as a
midshipman (and upper ranks) in his *Fragments of Voyages
and Travels,* and there is a good selection of the
autobiographical portions of those in *The Midshipman; being
autobiographical sketches of his own early career, from
Fragments of Voyages and Travels* (1862).

The following contents have been transcribed from the
United Service Journal Part III, 1831, and Parts I, II and III,
1832. The original spelling has been preserved. The first
obituary notice is taken from Part I of 1833. Footnotes that are
in italic have been added by the editor; the chapters correspond
to the different issues of the journal in which they were
published; there are not necessarily logical breaks between
them.

Recollections of a Sea Life

CHAPTER I

ABOUT two years after the death of my father, a respectable old officer, who knew my family, was appointed to command a ship, which was to be fitted out for the express purpose, as he supposed, of being employed with the North Sea fleet. The name of this sort of home service reconciled my mother to accede to my wish of going to sea; though, indeed, the kind old lady never could refuse anything that I persisted in. Accordingly, in April 1795, I joined His Majesty's ship G— in company with two other young *protegés* of the Captain.

The ship was not yet out of the hands of the dock-yard authorities. No men had been appointed to her, and although the officers had been appointed, they had not yet joined. Our Captain, who had come from Scotland at the same time as ourselves, in order to take command, desired us to remain on board, rightly judging that three raw Scotch boys were better there than cruising about Deptford. This was tiresome enough, but the scene soon changed. The continued hammering of the caulkers and other artificers from the dock-yard, was mixed with the bustle of more general preparation. The First-Lieutenant joined; some draughts of men were supplied to the ship; and a party of Greenwich pensioners were allowed to work on board at daily hire. The operations were no longer upon the mere hull; the more complicated duties of preparing the whole machine began their progress.

The two youngsters already mentioned, and myself, were the only persons in the shape of officers, whom the First-Lieutenant, when he joined, found on board; so that, although we were ignorant of every thing, we were immediately put in requisition as his assistants, and sent off in boats with messages, or appointed to the charge of little parties of the men who were employed to get in the ballast at the lower-deck ports. I was highly pleased with the importance which this kind of command gave, and became anxious to get as much as possible done by the party in my charge. I divided them for this purpose into two parties, and endeavoured to excite emulation between them. The men, pleased or amused with their young officer, entered into the spirit of the thing, and tried which could get in most. Of course I fancied my own charge of more consequence than any thing else that was going on, and when all hands were called upon deck for some other duty, I remember running up to ask the First-Lieutenant if my parties might be spared, for I had got "a *strive* established between them." In this way we went on fitting out in the fine weather of a fine summer, in the river Thames, and I thought the sea-life the happiest possible; while my imagination was excited to its glories by the tales of the Greenwich pensioners, to whom I listened with avidity at every leisure hour.

It was late in the autumn before we were ordered round to Spithead, to make one of a large fleet which was then beginning to assemble, to form an expedition for an attack on the enemy's colonies in the West Indies. The fleet were under the orders of Admiral Christian[1]. On our arrival at Spithead, in H M. S. G— her lower deck guns were ordered to be dismounted and put down in the hold, to make room for some of the troops, which it was intended should be embarked on board of her, to save, so far, the expense of hiring transports. Her guns were to be remounted on her arrival in the West Indies. She was peculiarly adapted for this kind of service, being one of those capacious Indiamen which were purchased for the navy about this time, and fitted out as men-of-war. Our Captain, however, thought it derogatory to him that his ship, commanded by an old officer, should be so employed.

That any employment must be honourable which could save to the country the expense of hiring one transport, or more, while, with the saving, the required service could be much better performed, involves a principle that was not so well understood in those days, as it has been since the time when Lord St. Vincent carried the extreme of the maxim so far, as to employ captains in their barges to pick up floating pieces of oakum. This reference is sufficiently intelligible to my naval friends, as relating to one of those extreme measures by which Lord St. Vincent sometimes caricatured the orders he gave out, that he might thereby insure their being made clear to the dullest capacity. To the uninitiated, the reference may require explanation.

---

[1] *Hugh Cloberry Christian, 1747-1798. The fleet embarked November 16, 1795*

2

Before the time when Lord St. Vincent exercised a powerful sway over the naval service, and freely used his "*hatchet*"[1] to cut down all sorts of innovations and abuses, particularly in the civil departments of the service ; and, for such purpose, it must be confessed that this instrument was better adapted than the "*penknife*" with which Lord Nelson cut through the obstacles that lay between him and an enemy; before this time, I say, the preservation of the stores, supplied for the use of the navy, was not attended to with that care that so important a branch of the service demanded. Zealous officers there were who did attend to those matters, but it was not so much the fashion for captains to be conversant in them then as it became afterwards, and as, I believe, it continues to be, so that they themselves supervise every expenditure, and cause the stores to be nursed and husbanded; and when worn out for one service, to be applied to another, in such a way, that not a rope-yarn of the old cable shall be lost, through the gradations of small rope, spun yarn, &c. until it is finally exhausted in oakum to caulk the seams with. Previous to this time, for instance, many small ends of rope-yarns, which were cut off in working them up, only added to the load for the scavenger's basket, which grows in a most unaccountable manner every hour, and is thrown overboard as often as the decks are swept. Or, if such shakings were not allowed to be thrown overboard, they were often kept for the much more injurious purpose of allowing the boatswain to exchange them for brooms to sweep the decks with, of which it was asserted the supply from the dockyard was not sufficient. The boatswain could always find some waterman, who came off to the ship, ready for this kind of barter. This, of course, opened the way to a temptation for him to inclose valuable rope among his shakings, and to receive something more than brooms in return. The shameful laxity in the civil department also made it a very easy matter for Mr. Boatswain to settle this business with the clerks at the dockyards, who took an account of returned stores; so, when a survey was held on his remains, they were found to be all right.

To remedy such abuses, many orders were given out by Lord St. Vincent, when he commanded the fleet; and many regulations were made by him when he was afterwards First Lord of the Admiralty. Among the orders he issued to the fleet,

---

[1] See Capt. Basil Hall's "Fragments," vol i, page 169.

this was one—that every ship should have attached to each mast, between the decks, and also on the quarter-deck and forecastle, a canvass bag to receive the shakings, which were to be carefully gathered every time the decks were swept. The use for which the bag was made, was also to be painted upon it.

Another circumstance connected with the incident which I am about to mention is that there was some peculiarity in the manner in which Lord St. Vincent used to lay the fleet to, when it was necessary for the ships to communicate with the flag-ship, or with each other. Instead of laying the main-top-sail flat aback, and the helm a turn a-lee, in the old-fashioned way, he was fond of keeping steerage-way upon the ships, not letting them drive like mere hulks, but keeping them going through the water, fast enough to be under control of the helm. The object probably was to enable them better to preserve their relative position to each other, and to be more ready on the instant to perform any evolution. It was also a very handy way of giving a boat a good long row in a cold morning , particularly if the captain, who might be in her, had added to its length, by having his ship further astern than she ought to have been, in which case, a small touch of the weather-helm and the lee-main-brace might keep the boat riding for any length of time. I should also mention, that about this time, the fashion of captains going in their state-barges upon all occasions, was beginning to wear out, with the gold-headed cane of the doctor on shore. And of this change his Lordship approved so much, that it was alleged these twelve or fourteen-oared boats always had a longer row than a four or six-oared boat.

Now, the story is, that shortly after the promulgation of the order about the shakings-bags, the captain of one of the ships in the fleet, who was endeavouring to get on board the flag-ship, was in his barge, rowing under the stern, while Lord St. Vincent was on the poop, looking out upon his fleet, or pacing the deck with his glass under his arm, and now and then casting a glance over the stern, to watch the progress of the barge, as she gained slowly on the ship. In doing this, his eye caught sight of a piece of rope-yarn, about two inches long, loosened into oakum, floating on the water, and which appeared to have come from his own ship. He hailed the barge, to let the Captain know of the impending loss of this part of the King's stores, and ordered that the piece of oakum should be picked up. The bowman laid in his oar, and reaching over the bow of the boat, caught the oakum between his finger and thumb, and held it up, but would not lift it into the boat.

" It is dirty, Sir!" to his Captain.

" It is dirty, my Lord," repeated the Captain.

" Wash it, Sir; wash it, Sir."

The oakum was washed, and brought on board the flag-ship, where it was deposited in the quarter-deck shakings-bag, at the main-mast, with all proper care.

But, to resume my narrative. The navy had not yet profited by this illustration of the maxim, that all service must be honourable by which the country can be benefited; so our Captain was very angry about the lower-deck guns being put in the hold, and resigned his command. Of course he was never employed again.

This truly benevolent and respectable man had been a very active officer in his youth, but he had not been employed between the time of the first war with America and that of his present appointment. In the interval he had got about him a rising family of ten children; and though willing enough to take his chance in the North Sea, it is probable that he did not like the prospect of dying ingloriously of the yellow-fever,– however advantageous such a result might have been to Junior officers, who would have profited by the vacancy in all the gradations from the post-captain downward.

He left us, however, and thus I lost my early patron and friend. Before he left the ship, he recommended that another youngster, of whom he had also taken a particular charge, and myself, should be removed into a smaller ship, "That we might be made to learn our duty better." In a large ship there are generally so many midshipmen, that it is a task for the first-lieutenant to find employment for them, to keep them out of mischief. In a small one, there are or were so few, that they must all be made useful in some way. In consequence of this recommendation, we joined H. M. S. P— attached to the same fleet as my former ship, namely, that under Admiral Christian.

I may mention here that the midshipmen's mess in the ship I now joined, consisted of a mate, two midshipmen, a captain's clerk, and a surgeon's mate (for we had no assistant-surgeon in those days). They were all grown-up men, and as the First-Lieutenant did not think their manners very exemplary, he very kindly and considerately put the other youngster and myself to mess with the gunner, a veteran seaman, from whom we heard nothing worse than some superstitious notions about foretelling the weather by the phases of the moon, and according to whether she set upon her back with her horns turned up: this last was a sure symptom of bad weather. Also, among some true stories of venerable date, I remember the one that gave rise to a saying often used by sailors when they would express a violent contest or struggle, "Pull devil—pull baker." The story is, that a merchant- ship, (of which my sage informant had the name, as well as the names of her owners, master, and crew,) had been supplied with very bad biscuit by a certain baker in London. During the passage outward to Smyrna, her crew had been very sickly, by reason of the bad biscuit; and while there, she had buried some of her men, from a continuance of the same cause. On her passage home, she met with bad weather, and put into some port in Italy. Having sailed from thence, she was becalmed under Mount Stromboli. While lying there becalmed, her Captain saw a figure like the wicked baker, on the verge of the burning crater. He appeared to be struggling hard with somebody.

As the smoke from the mountain spread itself, so as to inclose the ship, the captain could make out the person of the baker distinctly; and was also able to discover that of his opponent, who was no less a personage than the old devil himself. The object of the devil was to pull the baker into the crater of Mount Stromboli, while the baker, as he could not free himself from the grasp that had been laid on him, endeavoured to pull his satanic majesty from his strong hold. The victims of the baker's knavery in the mean time regarded the contest with eager delight; at first, highly pleased to see him in so fair a way of meeting with his deserts; but when he appeared to make a good fight of it, they forgot all their vindictive feelings; and in the true English spirit of fair play, cheered on the combatants, clapping their hands and vociferating - "Pull devil—pull baker!" as each in his turn made a good struggle for the mastery. The baker fought well. But in such a contest the event could not long be doubtful. When the devil found he had such a *"tough-un"* to deal with, he put forth a little more of his mettle, and soon dragged the poor baker over the edge of the crater, and plunged along with him into the raging gulf, that boiled with rising fury to receive them. The satisfactory evidence that they had not been deceived by the vision, was, that on the arrival of the ship in London, they found that the baker had died, and, of course, gone to the devil at the very hour that they had beheld his plunge into the volcano of Mount Stromboli.

With regard to my good messmate's notion, that the moon's being seen to set on her back is an omen of bad weather, it is much more easy to reconcile it to truth than the idea of the influence of her changes on the weather, which has been handed down from generation to generation, in opposition to the evidence of continued experience. In this climate, the prediction of bad weather will prove true three times out of four. This amount of accuracy in the practical result is more than sufficient to satisfy the disciple of a preconceived theory. Now the crescent of the young moon always sets upon her back;[1] and as the prediction of bad weather, *"more or less,"* is so generally a safe one, it is safe when the moon can be seen to go clown upon her back; that is, when the growing moon can be seen to set.

The converse of this proposition is, I imagine, assumed, although we never hear it expressed; namely, that it is an indication of fine weather, when the moon is seen to go down with her horns foremost, and her back up. Now she does so only when, being on the wane, she is reduced to a crescent, and in this case she sets under a shining sun; whereas the crescent of the increasing moon sets after the sun is gone down. It therefore happens, that the setting of the waning moon, when she is reduced to a crescent, is not observed; and, therefore, good weather is not predicted, which it ought not to be, in this country, by any prophet who has a respect for his prophetical fame.

This is more remarkably the case in the spring of the year; because, at this time, the declination of the growing moon, when first seen, is more northerly than that of the sun.

Now, I hope, I have satisfactorily proved, not only the theory we set out with, but also the converse thereof; and I feel that I have, therefore, some right to demand of other theorists on the moon's influence on the weather, that they should prove their's. But a very requisite preliminary to the proving of a theory is the enunciation of it. Now, it is a most curious matter to consider, that although some notion of the moon's ruling influence on the weather is so general as to be almost universal, yet there is not one in a hundred of those who maintain this notion, that can give a clear definition of their own belief in the nature or effects of that power. To the vague notions that cannot be expressed, there can, of course, be no answer. It is demanded, "why should not the moon have an influence over the weather, as well as over the tides?" To this I answer, that I do not pretend to say that she should not. All that I assert is, that no such power is reconciled to any known or recognised law of nature; and that, in point of fact, the observations on which it is assumed *are not made*. Few will ask the above question who have satisfied themselves of the truth of Newton's problem of the three bodies, by following his demonstration; and have then considered the moon's and earth's centres as two of those bodies; and a particle of water on the earth's surface, as the third body. To those who have not, it may be answered, that the amount of the moon's influence, as having a tendency to make a wave of the atmosphere analogous to the lunar wave of the ocean, is known and appreciated; but that it is so small, compared with the chemical causes which act upon the atmosphere, particularly those of heat and cold, by the expansions and contractions which they cause, that its effects are not perceptible upon the currents of air or winds. If it were otherwise, its effect should follow the diurnal periods of the moon; which is rather more than what is asserted by her most devoted disciples.

We now come back to the advantage of having an enunciation to our theory. I have sometimes known the attempt to make one turn out to be a cure for the belief. But if, after reducing the theory to an intelligible form, any one shall believe that he can predict the change or continuance of any sort of weather from the changes of the moon, let him, after writing down his theory, keep a written account of the weather for twelve months, and compare them. I will answer for his conversion, or be ready to investigate his theory and observations in order to be convinced; unless the theory be of that vague sort, that anything or everything may be made to agree with it. This plan of writing down what is believed and what is observed, seems the more necessary as even the learned Dr. Hayley was led by the almost universal voice on this subject, to suppose that the changes of the moon had an observable influence on the weather. He drew up a formula for predicting the weather, which depended chiefly upon the hour of the day at which the moon changed. Thus, making the weather at any place depend upon the longitude. The advantage of this process to Dr. Hayley was, that upon trial he found that the theory was untenable, and he abandoned it altogether. But many have heard of this formula, who do not know that it was renounced by its author.

Among the various modifications of this said influence of our lunar satellite upon the weather, I have heard the following statements. "When the moon changes, we shall have a change of weather." "If, when the moon changes, we have a change of weather, we shall have the weather that then comes for the whole of that moon," &c. Again, some are contented to attribute this power to the change of the moon; some to the full and change, and some to the days of her entering into her four quarters—a day or two before, or a day or two after. These last are pretty sure to be right, in the endeavour to reconcile their theory with observation; for they have two thirds of the time wherein to look for a point at which the weather may be suitable to compare with the other third, for the purpose of this reconcilement; so that being able to demonstrate the truth of their theory by undeniable observation, I fear that, like my good friend the gunner, this class of believers cannot be converted. Those who have taken up some of the other notions on trust, may be, if they will try the proposed experiments.

The ensuing winter was one of more violent and continued storms than any I have seen since; and now began my turn to be broken in for the realities of a sea-life. I well remember the day when I first found out that a sailor's profession required a greater portion of patient endurance and attention than I had yet been called upon to give it. I discovered what my late captain meant by being made to learn my duty m a small ship.

The signal was made for the fleet to weigh, in order to rendezvous at St. Helen's, as a more ready place to start from than Spithead. We had to beat down in a raw, cold day, blowing fresh with a drizzling rain. I was stationed to take charge of the crossjack-braces; and as I had learned the distinction between starboard and larboard, and knew the difference between letting go a rope, and pulling upon it, I thought I had my lesson perfect. There were certain other sounds which I had not yet learned to connect with my charge; such as-"Shiver the mizen topsail," "main-topsail haul," &c. But by a few sharp ratings from the first lieutenant for my stupidity, and being assisted by the superior knowledge of the men under my' orders, I soon learned to be of some use at this business, as long as I could fix my attention; but this habit I had yet to learn. Whenever there was a cessation for a few minutes, I found myself wandering from the spot in which I should have remained, to look at some of the hundreds of vessels passing and repassing, among which we were threading our way, beating out between the Horse and Dean and the Warner Sands, luffing for one, bearing up for another, heaving all aback for a third.

I was not allowed to remain long in these reveries. The now well- known sound of "shiver the mizen-topsail," recalled me, to find that I was in a scrape which threatened a four hours' spell at the mast-head. After four or five hours of tacking and backing and filling, we anchored at St. Helen's, amidst a wood of masts. On the morning of the — day of November, the wind had made a treacherous show of coming round to the north-east. The admiral made the signal to weigh.

After the usual delay of waiting for the ill-managed portion of the transports and merchant ships, many of which had boats on shore contrary to orders, and the usual repetition of signals, and expense of powder to enforce them, this immense fleet was under way. The men-of-war, the transports, with ten thousand troops and their appointments, and a large convoy of merchant ships, made the fleet amount to more than 300 sail. We could steer our course down Channel with the wind something to the eastward of north. This questionable sort of fair wind continued during the night, and in the afternoon of the next day we were in sight of the Promontory, which forms the western limit of Torbay, called Berry Head. The wind was then freshening up from the north-west, and continuing to back, (or shift its direction from right to left, contrary to the apparent diurnal motion of the sun) which is looked upon as ominous of bad weather. It now came from the west and was rising to a gale. The ships of war could have fetched into Torbay, which has famous shelter from a westerly wind; but, fortunately, the body of the fleet was too far to leeward to fetch into this bay; for had we anchored there, the devastation that followed, dreadful as it was, would have been woefully outdone.

Just before the closing in of a November day, the Admiral made the signal to bear up for St. Helen's, the rendezvous we had left. Before it became dark, the fleet had time to wear, and to stand up channel, under their close-reefed main-top-sails and fore-sails, with the wind from the south-west, ominously backing to the southward and blowing harder and harder. As the night closed in, this perverse changing of wind still continued until it came from the south and south-south-east; from whence it blew a furious tempest, with that pitchy darkness made by the mass of water in the air, well known to sailors by the name of scud, while it yet retains the place of a low fringy cloud ; but which now, joined with the surface of the sea blown into foam, formed one thick veil within which all was hidden.

I must here make a slight digression to give to such as are unacquainted with these matters, a clearer view of the circumstances of the fleet thus embayed upon a lee-shore. A little consideration will make it evident, that, although a ship, by setting her sails obliquely between the direction of the wind and that of her own length, may be impelled by the action of sails so set, in the direction of her length, not only at right angles to the wind, but with some oblique inclination towards the point from whence it blows; yet, if the wind becomes so violent that the sails which produce this effect must be taken in, the pressure of the gale upon the mere hull and rigging will tend only to drive her sideways before it. In the most violent gales, however, by the yards on which the sails are furled being braced obliquely, and by the form of the ship's bottom, she is enabled to make a course, not exactly side- ways before the wind, but one somewhere between that course and the point to which her head is directed. With all sail set, and smooth water, the true course which a ship makes through the water will deviate but little from that to which her head points, or *looks up for*, as it is called ; but as the sail is reduced, and as the waves become higher, the deviation of the true course made, from the line indicated by the direction of her head, becomes greater. This angle of deviation is called *lee-way*; and a ship is said to make one, two, three, &c. points of lee-way according as the true course she makes through the water is one, two, or three points to leeward of that which her head looks up for. The technical anomaly which makes this term difficult to be understood by a landsman is, that the term way when thus compounded, (*lee-way*) has no reference whatever to the *rate* or *velocity* with which the ship goes; but refers wholly to the *angle* above described.

The commencement of the tempest which I have mentioned, caught the fleet between the Bill of Portland and the Berry Head. The men-of-war and some of the weatherly transports were yet hardly within the line which would connect those headlands; but, by reason of the broad angle of lee-way which they made, the most weatherly had now no prospect of rounding the Bill of Portland on the one tack, or the Berry Head, with the Start Point stretching yet to windward of it, on the other. The more leewardly ships were already within the extensive bay, which is bounded by those headlands; and drawing near to the fearful lee-shore that extended itself between them. The tempest, now obstinately fixed in the south, continued to blow with unabated fury; and the fleet, thus caught, continued to drive towards this exposed coast, on which the foaming sea rolled its last outrageous burst, while the wasted water of the preceding wave was thrown back to swell the wild commotion of the next.

When the Admiral deemed the fleet to have drawn near enough to the Bill of Portland, I believe the signal was made to *wear*;[1] but it was literally a signal made to the winds. No ship could see another at the distance of twice her own length; and the noise of the tempest made the report of guns as inaudible as their flash was invisible. Each ship was, therefore, in perfect darkness as to the position of those around her: and, as the signal to wear was not heard, each wore according to her own reckoning, to make one more effort to avoid the nearest side of the bay in which we were thus engulfed, before she should reach her fate. In doing this, as she wore and stood to the westward, each had to perform the blindfold ordeal of threading her way among those which continued on the other tack. The anxiety to avoid collision with others was sufficiently on the stretch in all. The signal lanterns were kept lighted, and in readiness to have their covers pulled off, in order to be shown whenever it might be useful. "A good look-out before, there," from the quarter-deck, was answered every two minutes by "Ay, ay, Sir!" from the fore-castle and lee-gang-way. In about a quarter of an hour after we had wore, the look-out-man on the fore-castle called out " A ship close a-head, Sir" " Hard a-port."[2] "signal men, two lights at the weather-cat-head !" "Man the mizen- stay-sail, down-haul!" were three orders given by our excellent first lieutenant, in one breath, but with that loud, clear voice, and that distinct stop between each, that made the party to which each was addressed, feel that they were called upon for instant exertion.

For a time the helm had no effect; but as the mizen-stay-sail came down, our ship gradually fell off, and the figure of the other began to open on the weather-bow, lowering through the darkness with two lights at her lee-cat-head, to show that she was doing the right thing; while, by degrees, we fell off, and passed slowly to leeward of her, but so near, that each wave on which she rose, seemed as if it would launch over us the black mass which encumbered it. Some were not so fortunate. One

---

[1] In fine weather, when ships go about from one tack to the other, they tack; that is, they go round with their heads towards the wind, until they bring it on the other aide. If the water be smooth, and the operation be well managed, no ground is lost in this process. When there is a gale of wind and a high sea to contend with, ships cannot do this; and are, therefore, in that case obliged to wear;; that is, to put before the wind, and from that position to haul up to the wind on the other tack. In doing this a good deal of ground must be lost.

[2] The rule of the road is no paradox at sea, If you keep to the right you do *not* go wrong

ship was run down by another that remained to make the sad tale known. Others that came in contact went down together; and, though not in silence, at least with no noise that could vie with the tempest that roared over, and left oblivion in the place where they had been.

Thus we went on, making our leeward course to the north-east on one tack, and to the north-west on the other, and by every stretch, still narrowing the limit of the next, and drawing nearer to the fatal coast on which each hour brought some "poor devoted bark" to perform a new and short-lived tragedy. A white line of breakers now glared through the darkness; the hollows between the waves became deeper, and their towering heads more precipitous. One thundering bounce upon the ground gave a brief warning. One upward heave towards the steep beach, and the crashing backward-fall upon her broadside with the retiring surge, presented her decks to the next impending sea that burst upon them, and carried the shattered wreck of some good ship in its foam, while each following wave dashed the broken fragments on the beach, and swept them back to be again tossed by the next in restless succession.

The short day which followed saw a repetition of such scenes, and another black night, which promised their still more frequent recurrence, was soon to close in. About two o'clock, however, our ship could carry her fore-sail and main-top-sail. They were accordingly set. About four o'clock, some rain fell. The wind lulled, but piped up again in a strong gale from the north-west. The clouds began to break, and to assume that compact form and defined edge which makes what sailors call "a hard sky." The red glare of sunset shone through them. "All hands make sail," announced the glad tidings, for all were pretty well aware of the scrape we had been in. "Away up ! loose the fore and mizen-top-sails :" "Away up! loose the main-sails" "Shake one reef out of the top-sail ;" were now the orders that gave promise of weathering the Bill of Portland.

Next morning opened to smile upon the ruin that had been made; and saw the remainder of the fleet sailing up Channel, scattered far and wide, but all with their fine weather canvas spread. Our little ship being the repeating frigate, (a sort of aid-de-camp to the Admiral's ship,) was despatched to all quarters to repeat the Admiral's signals for calling them together, and that evening we anchored at St. Helen's.

At the dawn of the following day, a signal was made, which called our Captain on board the flag-ship; and another which warned us to prepare to weigh. Our Captain soon returned, and as he stepped on board, pronounced the words, "Up anchor!" In a quarter of an hour we were standing out to round Bembridge Ledge; and in an hour we were standing down Channel, with a clear sky, an easterly breeze; and, as we reeled merrily along, startling the sea-birds that were now riding on the rippling waves. We arrived in Portland Roads that evening. A person came off, who gave us the information we had come for, which consisted of the names of the lost ships, as far as they had yet been ascertained by fragments which bore them; with the melancholy addition that five hundred dead bodies had been picked up the preceding days, in a line of about four mile of the beach west of Portland; but we could not hear of any living thing that had been saved.

CHAPTER II

EARLY next morning, we sailed with the melancholy details of the fate of our late convoy; and with a rattling gale of wind from the westward, reached St. Helen's that night. New troops and transports were appointed to supply the place of those which had been lost, and we waited here until they joined us. Outward-bound merchant-ships were added to the convoy, until our fleet consisted of about the same number as had formerly sailed. Late in November, or early in December, for I do not recollect which[1], the wind once more came from the north-east, and again the fleet steered down Channel with a fair wind. It soon shifted, and again blew hard from the westward. By taking advantage of its changes between the north-west and south-west, however, we managed to get down Channel, and about as fur to the westward as the 18th degree of longitude, and as far south as the 43rd or 44th degree of latitude. Here, however, all efforts failed to advance us further. On some days we had gained ten or twenty miles to the south or west, but we more frequently found ourselves twenty or thirty miles to the north-east of our place on the preceding day.

Under the severe sickness I suffered during most of this time, one of the liveliest recollections I have, is that of seeing our boatswain drink off half-a-pint of brandy, and envying the zest with which he did it. I was tired of the wet and cold of the deck, to say nothing of the mast-head, where I had been perched to count the convoy; and had been relieved from the deck at twelve o'clock, the end of my watch. I could not eat my dinner of salt pork; and had come out from the gunner's cabin, which was in a corner far from the hatchway, about six feet in length and breadth, and *four feet three inches* in height. I had come out from this place to get a little fresh air, and had fixed myself at the foot of the ladder at the after-hatchway. It was Christmas-day, and our Captain, not very wisely, chose to commemorate it by sending a half-pint of brandy to each of the three warrant officers, the boatswain, gunner, and carpenter,

---

[1] *December 9th.*

16

to put into their plum-puddings. For this good purpose it was
rather late, even if the parties receiving it had been disposed
so to apply it. Something had called the boatswain on deck at
this time, and when he arrived at the foot of the ladder, he met
the Captain's steward with the brandy and message. "I'll tell
the plum-pudding when I come down," says the boatswain;
"Here's the Captain's good health." So saying, he gulped it
down and jumped upon deck. I did envy him, and thought him
the cleverest fellow alive.

It was not long after this that I got clear of my sea-
sickness. It had stuck by me during more continued trials than
any instance I remember to have seen; although I have heard
of people being continually liable to it. I had finished another
forenoon watch upon deck, and descending to the gunner's
cabin, attacked the salt junk and dough-boy with a keen
appetite; but the closeness of the place and the heaving of the
ship were too much for me. I had scarcely time to get on deck
to make my offering to Neptune in the manner approved of in
such cases. After five minutes more on deck, the hungry feeling
returned. My indulgent messmate, the gunner, allowed me
another dinner. I eat up a doughboy and a piece of salt beef,
drank off a glass of grog of his making, went immediately upon
deck, and I have never been sea- sick since.

Whenever the clearness of the weather permitted its being
done, the men-of-war were dispatched in all directions to collect
the straggling ships of the convoy. By such means, the convoy
were, at times, collected into a pretty compact body; but then
came a succession of gales of wind, with thick weather, which
caused their dispersion, so that, when our view was again
extended, the number of ships to be counted from the masthead
was much diminished. Some were more weatherly than the
rest, and went out of sight a-head, or to windward. These
pushed on, and a few of them, thus relieved from waiting on
the motions of the dull-sailing and leewardly ships, arrived at
the appointed rendezvous in the West Indies. Those which
parted company to leeward, continued to drive more and more
to the northeast, until, for want of water, they were obliged to
bear up for the Cove of Cork, or into the Channel again. Some
were compelled to do so from losing their masts by the violence
of the wind ; or by running foul of each other by night. And

some, I fear, went down in this way. From all these circumstances, however, the number of the convoy was reduced from above three hundred to about seventy in five weeks.

Before the end of the sixth week, the convoy being thus reduced, and the transports falling short of water, and there being no appearance of a change of weather, it was thought right to return to port to collect the force and recruit the supplies of the expedition. The signal was once more made, to bear up for St. Helen's. We bore up with a strong gale from the west-south-west, and in three days arrived at St. Helen's: thus running back in three days all the distance we had made in six weeks. I believe that the vigilance and attention of H. M. S. P—, as repeating ship, was noticed by the Admiral, and, in addition to this, our Captain was a man of good family interest, so that, although a very young man, he was appointed to command a better ship. He was pleased to take three midshipmen with him, of whom were the youngster who had accompanied me from the G— and myself. One circumstance which gave me great pleasure in this change was, that our excellent First Lieutenant, Mr. B— , was to go with us. He still lives, and, I trust, continues to enjoy the rank and the retirement which he has so well earned. One of my first feelings of ambition was, that I could become such an officer as that man; and if I have never done so, I am conscious that I have, at least, benefited by keeping such a model in my recollection. Since I am about to leave H. M. S. P—, I may as well make a farewell description of her.

During these foul-weather cruises, the men had neither dry clothes nor bedding for two days together. If mine were ever dry at all, it was owing to the disinterested care of the captain of the forecastle, a Newhaven fisherman and pilot, who, because the two youngsters were Scotch boys, took an interest in us similar to what Tom Pipes did of Peregrine Pickle. Besides the good office of hanging up the contents of our chests and hammocks to dry whenever there was an opportunity, he also took some trouble to teach us the art of knotting and splicing, in lieu of the games which Pipes, in his days of idleness, taught his pupil. It was in consequence of this friendly man's advice, also, that I learned to obviate any bad effects which this amphibious kind of life might have had upon the health, by dispensing with the use of sheets. This I did the more readily, as his advice was coupled with some caustic remarks upon so effeminate a practice as that of using them. Long afterwards I found the advantage of dispensing with this luxury during the intense cold of a Baltic or North-sea winter.

But to return to the description of H. M. S. P—, The sailors used to call her the coffin, and certainly she had a resemblance to one. She was painted black, which makes a ship look small; and sets off to advantage the lofty appearance of her masts, that tower over those of any merchant-ships of her own size which happen to be near her, and adds to her warlike appearance. Some officers are fond of the rakish pirate-like look which this mode of painting gives, assisted by red portsills, &c. The P— was, or rather had been, black, and all black; but being somewhat rickety, the pitch and oakum had worked out of her seams, and the brown oakum where it protruded, and the brighter marks of red rust of iron that oozed out of every bolt-hole, sadly disfigured her sable coating. The upright part of her hull, which rose above her line of guns, was high in proportion to that which rounded off below it; and this gave her that square, chest-like appearance, which made Jack's simile of a coffin rather appropriate, as, indeed, all his similes are; but in this I suspect he had a double meaning, relating to the probable use she might come to in conveying us to the bottom. She certainly was a bad sea-boat, used to ship a great deal of water, as well over all, as by the inlets of her rickety frame; and was altogether a bad specimen of French naval architecture, for such she was.

As she with the rest of the fleet got out to the West Indies on the third attempt, I have no doubt that my friend the Gunner was confirmed in a notion which he had taken up, that I was the Jonas on whose account we had had the bad weather. This arose from a passage in a letter from my mother which I had incautiously read to him. The poor old lady had already lost two sons in the West Indies; and when she consented to my going into a ship to be stationed in the North Sea, she had no idea of the facility with which naval destinations are changed. Accordingly, when she heard that we were about to sail for the West Indies, one of her letters expressed a prayer, that "adverse winds might drive us far from those pestilential shores." This passage I had incautiously read aloud in presence of my messmate, who could not afterwards be persuaded that the writer was not a witch – and the *incantation* contained in the letter met with many maledictions, whenever the lowering sky and rising swell gave tokens of another gale of wind to contend with. The ship was, however, now relieved from this source of enchantment.

His Majesty's ship A–, although not one of the large frigates, was a fine one of her class; and having been refitted since her last cruise, appeared in all the neatness of her new equipment. Her hull nicely painted; her dead-eyes, newly turned in, formed the lower termination of the rigging of each mast in an exact row, the evenness of which was not yet broken by the unequal stretching of the shrouds; her rigging newly tarred; her yards glossy with blacking, and her top-masts, topgallant-masts, and studding-sail booms newly scraped, and shining with grease.

The two ships lay near each other, and the rugged appearance of the one, and the gay trim of the other, as she rode like a duck upon the water, formed a strong contrast. On board the two ships, also, the contrast was favourable to the A—. There appeared to be room to move about her decks, and from the lower deck, where the habitation of the officers and men was, to the main-deck which formed its roof, there was a full foot more of height; so that when the rays of the sun found their way down the hatchway, some light was refracted from them towards the men's mess-berths, and gave a cheerful and airy appearance below. The midshipman's berth, however, did not partake of these occasional glimpses of day-light, being incased in a bulk-head, or boarded partition; but it was larger than that of the P–, and, as I mentioned before, a foot higher in the roof.

Our good first lieutenant, whose friendly care had sent me to mess with the gunner in the former ship, now permitted me to join the midshipman's berth in the A—. It did not correspond so nearly with a midshipman's berth of Smollet's days as that of the P— did ; but it did so more nearly than any which could be found in these refined days · degenerate days, Admiral Benbow would call them, if he could rise out of his grave.

At the time I speak of, the demand for midshipmen was greater than the supply of eligible candidates ; and while the notion entertained of a midshipman by people on shore was that of a smart little boy with a cocked-hat as big as himself, the real grouping of a midshiman's berth in those days was often made up of very motley materials, composed of all ages of men from fifty downwards.

Many were taken from before the mast. ·Where this was done in a direct manner there was sometimes a good reason for it; but the most general cause was the want of a sufficient number of fit persons to fill the ratings of midshipmen on the books. Many of the midshipmen thus made were never meant by the captain who promoted them, to be brought into the line of promotion to an admiral; but merely to have the *rating* of midshipmen in order to increase their pay. These were, sometimes, not put on the quarter-desk or into the midshipman's berth-at first; but then came another captain who did not approve of this anomalous state of things, nor did he choose to deprive the person of his place and rating without a cause; and as those promoted in this way were generally assiduous and useful in one way or another, there would have been injustice in doing so. Consequently, the useful person had tails added to his jacket, and took his place in the midshipman's berth.

The worst of this was, that the persons so promoted were not always seamen. One, and the worst source of this sort of indirect promotion, arose from giving the rating of midshipman to men who made themselves useful by being able to write a fair hand. These, often, had failed in some occupation on shore by drunkenness or other bad conduct, before they were reduced to enter in a man-of- war before the mast, and were the worst possible associates for young gentlemen. Of the midshipmen who served in the two ships which I have before referred to, while I was in them, I can only remember the names of two who ever attained the rank of lieutenant, and one who was made a master. Of the rest, some found their way back to the place they had come from, before the mast, some died, and, of the small remainder, some possibly were promoted at the Jubilee, or at the end of the war, when the Admiralty, in despair of being able to select among the conflicting claims of the multitude of midshipmen of ancient date, made a sweeping promotion on some general principle, which raked up from the hold and lower-decks some, whose duties had confined them to those regions until they had almost forgotten the colour of daylight; whose home was the cock-pit, and who could not easily be reconciled to a higher one.

Besides the injury suffered by the service from the irregular manner in which the place of future candidates for promotion was thus supplied, I have known serious injustice done to the men who were so advanced, by their being unfairly placed thereby in situations of trust, which their education and confirmed habits had unfitted them for, and who were made to suffer the penalty of a breach of the trust thus unwisely, and even unfairly, put upon them. Good men, also, who had been promoted into this line as a reward for some exemplary conduct, were excluded from reaping. any advantage from the reward, by the fact of their having come from before the mast being made a barrier to their passing the examination necessary to qualify for farther promotion; because the loose manner in which men had been taken from before the mast, made it difficult or impossible to discriminate. Such, at least, was believed to be the case by men standing in this situation, when I had an opportunity of seeing them in the short peace of Amiens, and it was probably so also, when the navy was again reduced.

A particular instance of this came within my notice at the former period, when I passed my own examination for lieutenant.

We had been absent on a voyage to China with a convoy, and, before our return, the three master's-mates, of whom I was one, had completed the time of service necessary to qualify for that examination; and in the interval the treaty of Amiens had been concluded. We all three, however, went to London in high glee, for the purpose of appearing at Somerset House, where such examinations were conducted at that time. From having given our names in early, they stood at the head of the list of candidates to be examined. My two messmates were the first and second, mine was the third.

After more than half an hour' anxious waiting for each, I saw my predecessors come out from the examining-room in their turn, with faces as long as the main-top-bow-line. They were both turned back. I supposed that they must have failed in some of the pen- and-ink business of navigation: but no - they had passed that ordeal and been ordered to stand up, and had gone through a long examination as to the management of a ship in various situations. They both stated to me that no objection had been made to any of their replies; and, from the circumstantial account which they gave, and other circumstances, I am quite sure that they answered all the questions satisfactorily; and that they owed their being turned back, merely to their having been promoted from before the mast, and to their being advanced to an age some where between thirty and forty.

By way of softening the repulse they thus met with, one was recommended to pass for a gunner, and the other for a boatswain; but after being led to look for promotion in the direct line to an admiral, they could not brook this. Besides, by the peace reduction, which was then contemplated, there was no prospect of their now being able to obtain the situation of boatswain or gunner, if they had passed, particularly as the captain who promoted them had retired. They accordingly left the service, and I do not know what became of them.

These two men had been placed on the quarter-deck by their well-meaning captain for good conduct during the mutiny at the Nore. Had they then been recommended to the situations of gunner or boatswain, they would have been rewarded, and the service would have profited; as it was, they met with a grievous disappointment, and the service lost two good men.

I am far from meaning that the line between the foremastmen and the officers should be made impassable; but while some captains held opinions almost amounting to this, there were others, who marked by their practice too great a disregard to the consequence of this kind of promotion; and, from mere whim, rated persons as midshipmen, who, although very good men in their place, had nothing to recommend them which gave promise of their ever being capable of the trust required to be placed in an officer; and who, accordingly, when it became their duty to supervise the issue of spirits to the crew, or in some other case, were guilty of a breach of trust, and sent back before the mast, with disgrace to themselves and discredit to the class into which they had been introduced.

The respect paid to this class of officer was already too little for any in that line which was hereafter to supply the higher rank of officers, because the want of respect to that class prevented those who were in it, and thus placed in the school for future admirals, from respecting it themselves, and thereby tended to lower the standard of morals and manners in it.

These effects appear to me to have arisen from two causes combined:

First, that the number of midshipmen allowed to the fleet, *when the war complement of ships was employed,* was greater than that of eligible candidates for the station; and it was also greater than the number necessary to keep up the supply of officers.

And, secondly, from the uncontrolled power of the captains to make and to break midshipmen.

In making these observations, I am quite aware that the regulations which have been made since the conclusion of the war, respecting the admission of midshipmen into the navy, and their dismissal from it, has corrected the evil I complain of; but it has done so when the mere reduction of the number of midshipmen allowed to the navy would alone have tended very much to do so. What I have said upon this subject is, therefore, chiefly for the purpose of introducing the remark, that those regulations will not be found of practical or efficient application, if the demand for persons to fill the station of midshipmen should again become greater than the supply of eligible candidates.

If ever the navy should be again employed in an extended numerical force, similar to what it was in the war, it may, therefore, become a question highly worthy of consideration, whether a reduction of the number of midshipmen allowed to the ships, and particularly to large ships, would not be attended with benefit to the service. I do not lose sight of the advantage of rearing in this class a supply of candidates for the place of officers which should be greater than the demand; but if this principle be carried to a useless extent, and if in following it the supply of future candidates be diluted with a great portion of unfit subjects, it becomes an evil instead of an advantage. This evil did certainly arise from the number of midshipmen allowed to the navy during the war. For although in ships commanded by men of rank, or of renown as officers, there was always a sufficient competition to fill the place of midshipmen; yet there was a large portion of ships in commission that could not ob-tain proper persons to fill those places, and therefore took such as they could get.

It appears quite clear, that if this very loose mode of collecting this class, which produced the future candidates for the place of officers, was found sufficient to supply a competent number of eligible candidates, besides a multitude from whom it was not easy to select; if the loose mode I have referred to produced all this, it may be inferred, that a smaller number admitted into the class of candidates would be found sufficient, if more care was taken in selecting for that admission.

The limitations which have been made on the Captain's power of entering and discharging midshipmen since the conclusion of the war, have been most wholesome, and it may be hoped that they would be found applicable in case of another war, which, I think, they would be if combined with the reduction of the number of midshipmen proposed above, but not without it.

Before those limitations took place, while the breaking of a midshipman was only the *irresponsible* fiat of one man, no disgrace followed the victim of it out of the ship in which he then was, provided that he had friends to get him into another. I have known two instances, at least, of midshipmen being turned out of their ships for very disgraceful conduct, whom I afterwards met in the shape of officers. I can also recollect the consolatory remark made by midshipmen when they got into some scrape and were threatened to be turned out of the ship, that "there were more ships than churches," thus showing their carelessness on the subject.

Now, however, that such a dismissal is not made without due publicity of investigation, it would meet with its proper share of odium, and the person so dismissed would be effectually weeded out from the number of future candidates for promotion.

The advantage to the service by the restrictions on the captain's power of making midshipmen has already been referred to. But besides the advantage to the service, an essential good will arise to such men as may be deemed worthy of this kind of promotion, upon proper representations, since their promotion would be an act of the Admiralty that would of course not fail to be duly recorded. Had my two good messmates, the master's mates abovementioned, being promoted into this class by an order from the Admiralty, upon proper representation of their good conduct in the mutiny, and their fitness in other respects, their names would, at least, have been enrolled on a list which would have prevented their being *shuffled* out of the service. That captains should be encouraged to make known to the Admiralty the merits of those whom they deem worthy of such promotions, will be admitted, when we call to mind numbers of men whose names do honour to the nation, and who have risen from before the mast.

Before I quit this subject I should like to record the name of one man, John Wilkie, who, had he lived, might have risen to such distinction. I have a most satisfactory recollection of my reports of this man having been instrumental to his promotion. The recollection might have been a proud one, had he lived to realize the promise he gave.

John Wilkie was a quarter-master on board H. M. S. B— in the West Indies, at the time that I was an acting lieutenant in her. The boats of this ship, at the time I speak of, were much employed near the land, or in calm weather, when the ship could not be made effectual, to enforce the blockade of the island of Martinique. In the course of this service they were frequently under the enemy's batteries; and among many vessels which they intercepted they attacked and captured two of the enemy's privateers. One of these was attacked and captured in the open day in a calm. Upon all these occasions John Wilkie was coxswain of the barge; and as the charge of particular boats, when employed upon this kind of service, and the exercising of their crews, was assigned to the different lieutenants respectively in this shjp, the barge was my charge, and I was generally in her when she left the ship. I had reason to be proud of the promptness and alertness of my boat's crew, and for this I was chiefly indebted to the zeal and ability of John Wilkie. His officer-like qualities, by showing an example to his men, had infused a spirit into them, which made all and each of them feel as great a pride in that promptitude as their officer could do. His orders to them, too, although he had not been used to command, were given in the true style of one who did know how, and had been accustomed to it. They were decided, and given in a manner which showed that instant obedience was expected and required, but never in the querulous or impatient style of- "Why don't you do this?" or "Why don't you do that?" To these good qualities he added the power of steering his boat with admirable cheerfulness of aspect under the fire of an enemy, and partaking of the jokes which were passed on their good or bad aim-taking. This was more remarkably observable in the case of the privateer taken in the calm, which was approached under a shower of grape and musketry. After taking this vessel he was promoted to be a master's-mate, and as this was at the commencement of a war, which had twelve years' duration, this promotion, if he had lived, might have brought him into a rank where his good qualities would have been better known. He died, however, soon after the event which I have mentioned – not that death to which he was always ready to expose himself · he died of the yellow fever. One more point in this man's character which I should notice, was his unaffected and *gentlemanly* demeanour when promoted, and invited to the table of his captain. He took his seat there, not only without awkwardness but with ease, and gave his opinion on subjects which called for it without bashfulness, but also wholly without that vulgar attempt at familiarity which is sometimes used as a cloak for it, and while his manners were perfectly respectful to everybody, there was not the least appearance of any consciousness of inferiority in himself, as there was certainly no ground for such a conciousness. In conversation it was easy to see that he had been all his life before the mast, not from any vulgarity in it, but because his references were all to scenes which he had witnessed in that situation.

If the view which I have taken of reducing the number of midshipmen allowed to large ships, when the number of ships is again increased to a war establishment, should ever be entertained by the Admiralty, they would, of course, not diminish the efficiency of the ships, by cutting off any portion of the number of their petty officers, but in reducing the list of midshipmen, they would extend to a corresponding number the other classes of petty officers who are not candidates for promotion, or who would be so only for the situation of warrant officers. Such an extension would add to the captain's power of promoting good men in a manner that would be beneficial to the service as well as to the men themselves, and thereby would add to the means of reconciling good seamen to the compulsory service in the navy which is required of them in time of war, without ·placing them in a situation to be educated for a new line of' life, after their habits are confirmed, which, it must be confessed, ought only to be done with careful discrimination.

By what has been said about the injury done to the cockpit as a school for those who were to become officers, it is by no means meant that it was, in fact, a bad school. Our fellow-countrymen are pleased to think that it has not been so in its general effect, but I would say that this is in spite of the evils I have referred to, and certainly not arising from them. The Navy, as well as the Army, as a school for young gentlemen, has always this great good belonging to it; that each one, in the society he moves in, is made to feel that be must depend for his place, as to consideration in that society, upon himself alone; and he feels also, that it is upon this consideration alone that he must depend for countenance. No adventitious aid of rank will obtain this for him in the cockpit. He is also removed from the means of being independent of this respect, by being closely tied up to the society of his fellows, and cut off from seeking the countenance of partial relations. All assumption of a feigned character, in the familiarity of the cockpit, no less than in the intimacy of the ward-room or press-room, is soon seen through; and as sterling worth never fails to command respect in any society where it is known, it becomes the standard which is aimed at.

The near contact of, and mutual dependence upon each other which prevails in actual service between the junior officers and men, also teaches officers better to feel their place as one of a community of mankind, and to know and appreciate the value, and the virtues or failings, of that class which is known, to young men brought up at home or in universities, only as the vulgar; a variety of the species whom they blindly suppose to be incapable of any feeling, or, at least, of any noble or generous feeling in common with them. Such notions are effectually corrected by witnessing the disinterested sacrifices which these men can make for each other, and more particularly for their officers, when circumstances arise calculated to call forth those feelings.

Our first cruise in the A—[1] was off the west coast of Ireland, with a fleet of men-of-war, and here we had no dull sailing merchant-ships or transports to trouble us. Our object was to intercept the Dutch fleet, which were reported to have left the Texel, and to be on their way to Brest, by sailing round the north of Scotland. I believe they put back to the Texel, as they were there next year, and got well beaten not many mile from it. They did not come our way this time, however, so we returned to Spithead after a month's cruise.

Our next expedition was to Quebec, to carry out a new Governor of Canada, and to bring back the former one. The most interesting event in this passage across the Atlantic, was the chace of an English letter-of-marque, who took us for a Frenchman, while we took him for one. In the end, there was the mutual disappointment, more agreeable to those on board the chace than to us; but the delight on board of her was so great, and expressed in so lively a manner, that it afforded us a new scene, which soon banished the recollection of our disappointment. Among a number of respectable-looking people who were passengers, joy was unboundedly expressed by many a cheer, and many a wave of handkerchiefs from fair hands, as we shot up close alongside of her, and hailed her in English, and they became assured that we were really an English frigate.

---

[1] *H.M.S. Active, 32 guns, Captain Edward Leveson-Gower. See Clowes, The Royal Navy, London, 1899 – Vol. 4, p. 549.*

We sailed so much better than she could, that she would have had no chance of escape from us in that way; so when we had come near enough to fire a shot over her, she hove to, and hauled down her English colours in token of submission, although ours were flying, so determined did her commander seem to take us for a Frenchman. A fresh fair wind was blowing; we had no time to lose, and the above-mentioned salutations and the answers to all questions being satisfactory, we made all sail, dashed by the ship of our fair friends like a dolphin, and soon lost sight of them and her.

After encountering a due portion of impervious fogs, and narrowly avoiding to run over some fishing-vessels which were lying at anchor, we passed the banks of Newfoundland, and as we approached the coast had to thread our way among numbers of ice-bergs, which had drifted thus far to the southward: this was in the month of May. Some of these ice-bergs were small, and for that reason more dangerous, because not easily seen at night, or during a fog; and as we had a fine breeze, and were going about eight knots, one of them would have made a hole in our bows as effectually as a rock. By a good look-out, however, or, perhaps, as Miss Edgeworth's Paddy says, "By the blessing of God, and our good-luck," we did not touch any of them. There was one very large, which had quite the appearance of an island. We could see many moving things upon it; they were chiefly seals; but those who were clever in their discernment, could perceive some white-bears among them, and persuaded their neighbours to see them also. Those who pronounced opinions about its height, said it was higher than our mast-head (140 feet) ; some said twice as high. It was of great dimensions, and its neighbourhood made the air very cold.

We lost our ice-bergs soon after we had made Cape Krace, the south-eastern promontory of Newfoundland, and sailing along the southern shore of that island with a fair wind, entered the Gulf of St. Lawrence. In crossing this gulf, we got sight of the long low island of Anticosta, not knowing that we were afterwards to form an acquaintance with it more intimate than agreeable.

We were several days in tiding up the "magnificent river St. Lawrence," and among other novelties, saw, near its mouth, many large porpoises of a milky whiteness; and approaching to Quebec, passed the Island of Orleans, with the fall of Montmorency tumbling over a precipice 240 feet high, into a bay at the back of this beautiful island, At Quebec we had time to get on board the necessary supplies, and for some other occupations and amusements, before the late Governor of Upper Canada, who was to return to England with us, was ready to embark. Lord — [1] with his family and suite, having embarked, we sailed and made our way down the river.

In the Gulf of St. Lawrence we met with foul winds and foggy weather; and as the setting of the currents in this gulf is liable to great variation, the navigation of it is dangerous in such weather. We had tacked off from the coast of New Brunswick, and had stood on upon the starboard-tack during the remainder of the night, with the wind about east-south-east, and the fog perfectly impervious to sight. The officer of the morning watch had orders to tack the ship at seven bells (half-past seven). The sand in the glass was nearly out. The hands were called about-ship, and were in their appointed stations for performing that evolution. There was a fine breeze, the ship going about five knots. The helm was ordered to be put down; but, before the order could be obeyed, the violent shaking of the ship, and a noise like thunder, announced that it was too late. The shelving rocks, dipping but slightly towards the sea, formed an inclined plane on which the ship made that hurling noise, as she launched upwards by reason of the impetus with which she had run on, until she was considerably raised upon this rock.

To heave the sails aback was the first effort which was naturally made; but the rate with which she had gone on, had given her much too firm a hold upon the rock to allow of this having any effect. The boats were then hoisted out, and preparations made for heaving her off by laying out anchors. The fog began to break, and we got some glimpses of the low wooded land close to the northward of us; soon afterwards the wind died away to a perfect calm. The sun shone out bright and

---

[1] *Lord Dorchester.*

hot, and the fog entirely disappearing, enabled us to discover our position. We were within about half a mile of the shore at the western end of the island of Anticosta, but a low shelving point projected from it towards us, and continuing to project under water, formed the rock upon which we were now stuck fast. The first efforts to heave the ship off were rendered futile by the anchors coming home. By reason of the smooth slaty nature of the bottom they took no hold in it; so that instead of the ship going to the anchor when the cable was hove upon, the anchor came to the ship.

Towards the afternoon, however, she was hove off by her last remaining anchor, and got into seven fathoms; but the want of anchors prevented her being able to warp farther from the land during the calm, to a situation from whence she could have beaten off against the strong breeze that followed; and the approach of which was already indicated by a rising swell that rolled to the shore. If any one shall suppose that there must have been some want of experience, some awkwardness in the exertions used, which prevented the ship from being got off farther from the danger in a whole day of calm weather, and some impatience, to cause the loss of all the anchors in getting her so far, I can only say that I knew nothing about those matters at the time; and as I cannot recollect now, even at what time it was high water, for there was some, but not a great ebb and flow, I do not feel qualified to give any opinion, but all parties were acquitted by a Court Martial, which investigated the question soon after the loss of the ship.

However, as the account I have given may raise a question among some officers of the present day, I feel it due to the gentleman who was the first lieutenant of the ship, and who was then an expert and experienced officer, as he is now an old and respected one of a higher rank – I feel it due to this officer to say, that the captain of the frigate[1] did not relinquish any share of that direction and command which his responsibility justified him in retaining; so that the efforts of the first lieutenant were confined to the execution of those orders.

---

[1] Leveson-Gower.

About six o'clock, light flaws of wind began to play in the water, and again vanishing, left the glossy smooth of a calm but undulating surface. Again, these treacherous breezes were seen upon the water and again vanished. The topsails and topgallant-sails were sheeted home and hoisted, (spread,) and the yards were braced about and about, to catch the first favourable air that might enable us to stand off from the land.

About eight o'clock, such a breeze came. The ship's head lay obliquely off the land with the after-yards braced up for the star-board-tack, and the sails full. The head-yards square. The cable was cut, the head-yards braced up, and all sail instantly made. Thus we appeared to be standing off the land, but the swell pre-vented our gathering headway. The cable had hardly been cut, when the wind fell lighter and came more a-head; and instead of making way off the land, we only did so sideways before the swell, and towards the ledge of rocks we had left – In this helpless sort of state, without an anchor to let go, and without wind enough to blow out a candle, the successive casts of the lead gave warning of the rapidly approaching fate of our nice little frigate- "By the deep six – quarter less six-and a half-five – and a quarter-five," &c., until with the announcement of – "And a quarter-three," we felt her stern touch as her head rose to the swell. The bumpings became more and more in earnest as the waves hove her farther on the rocks. Soon afterwards the sky overcast, and the wind began to whistle through the rigging with all the blustering appearance of a rising gale from the southward.

CHAPTER III

WE left H. M. S. A— in rather an awkward situation, beating on the rocks, with the night coming on, and a rising gale from the southward.

Since writing the account of her progress, indited from memory, at the distance of thirty-five years, I have been favoured with some memoranda written at the time, which enable me to mention the following particulars; viz. soon after she struck, the tide was found to be ebbing, and it was not high water again till near eight o'clock in the evening. It was not until this time, that the efforts to heave her off were effectual; she was then hove off into five and a quarter fathoms, *not seven*. The swell which had by this time risen, together with the flat smoothness of the rocky bottom, precluded the possibility of warping the ship farther out by any small anchor, and the swell also prevented the possibility of the boats now carrying out a large one. It was under these circumstances that, *at half-past nine,* it was deemed proper to cut the cable, and trust to the sails for weathering the reef. I find also, that the stream-anchor had been broken in heaving upon it, and that the sheet-anchor was remaining on board when the ship went on shore the second time. I presume, therefore, that the reason for its not being let go was, that when the wind came a-head, so as to make it impossible to weather the reef, she was so near, that, under the circumstances, the anchor could not have kept her from falling on it. · However, on it she went. The wind freshened. She now began to beat violently on the rocks, and, in the course of the night, became a complete wreck.

Soon after the ship had gone on the reef the second time, Lord — was prevailed upon to leave her; and a boat was sent with him to join his family, who had been previously put into a small fishing schooner that happened to be near. On the next day the weather became fine, but the destruction of the ship was by this time complete; and the water ebbed and flowed in her with the tide. The first lieutenant remained on board with a part of the crew, to send on shore such stores as could be saved; and, in the first place, provisions, with spars and sails to make tents.

A tent was, as soon as possible, got up for Lord —'s family, who were landed. The schooner was retained to be of what use she might. Tents were afterwards made for the men and officers. By working on board at low water, a sufficient quantity of provisions was got on shore to admit a full allowance of some articles, and half allowance of others, being served to the crew. There were some little helps to our short allowance, that we could not have had on board. After the first few days, there was less work to be done, so that we found time to make rambling excursions in quest of wild birds or fish. In the midshipmen's mess, we somehow or other got hold of a seal. I think, notwithstanding our short allowance, the flesh of the seal, in general, was not extolled, but the liver, &c. were declared to be equal to lamb's fry.

One day, when I had recommended myself to the first lieutenant by being on the alert while the work was going on at low water, I obtained his permission to take a run in the evening: so I got a powder-horn at my side, a load of bullets, cut into slugs, in my pockets, a ship's musket over my shoulders, and set off upon a solitary ramble along the coast, fancying myself a very Robinson Crusoe. In this reverie I had wandered several miles along the shore, and, as the sun went down, I was seated on a rock looking at his broad red disk, as it immerged behind the sparkling surface of a calm sea. When he was gone, however, I began to make the best of my way back to the tents, but it soon became dark, and the rough inequalities of the beach made my progress rather slow, so that it was late before I reached them. When I came within a mile or so, I heard some voices, and presently recognised that of my brother[1], (the youngster whom I have mentioned as having been removed with me from former ships,) who was rather younger than myself. Our friend the Newhaven fisherman was with him. As I approached them, I heard my brother crying bitterly, and I now began to fancy that I was the object of their search. I was not long left in doubt upon this subject, for the moment my brother saw me, he ran towards me, and snatching up the broken bough of a tree, gave relief to his feelings by discharging two or three hearty blows upon me. This novel

---

[1] *Lewis Campbell. Held rank of Commander as of 15 Nov. 1816.*

mode of expressing his joy and goodwill took me by surprise; but I was more disposed to laugh than to resent it, and we returned to the tents together. I found that his imagination had consigned me to the bears and wolves, the only inhabitants of the island.

After our immediate wants of tents and provisions had been supplied, the next consideration was, how to get from the island. We were about sixty miles from the nearest land of New Brunswick, and probably one hundred and fifty from any port where vessels were likely to be met with. I believe it was intended that our first lieutenant should go in the large cutter to search for some that would be able to take us off: our number was about 250. It was thought proper that the boat should be raised upon a streak before she was dispatched on this service. The carpenters were accordingly set to work upon her.

While these things were going on, a circumstance occurred which rendered it advisable to make some change in the arrangements. In the course of the proceedings above narrated, many of the men had shown a disposition to riot and mutiny. A marked instance of this occurred while the first lieutenant was engaged on board in endeavouring to save the stores and provisions. He was occupied in the lower parts of the ship, when information was brought to him that some of his men had broken open the lockers in the Captain's cabin, and were helping themselves to wine. He immediately jumped up among them, and his presence put some of them to flight; others were more restive, and stayed in defiance. One fellow, Patrick Roach, a great big Irishman, took up a cutlass, and put himself in an offensive posture. The first lieutenant promptly and gallantly seized another, and might easily have sent him down, although the Irishman was twice his bulk. The skill and activity of Lieut. B—, gave him a superiority, which he used with a forbearance and moderation but little merited by his adversary. Patrick Roach, made sensible of this superiority, laid down his arms, and was handed out of the cabin with the rest; the lockers were forthwith secured. This fellow was probably emboldened to act as he had done, by the knowledge of a combination, the plans of which were put in operation a few nights afterwards, when forty-five of the men entered the provision tent, loaded themselves, and carried off what they could to a place in the wood, to which they had already conveyed secretly such arms and ammunition as they could possess themselves of by stealth.

In all cases of rebellion or mutiny, as well as in such cases of reform as are carried by the display of physical force, it is well to remember, that the friends of good order, those who wish only for the redress of some real grievance, or relief from some real evil – in calling up that display, make common cause with those who have no common feeling with them, except in relation to the ostensible ground of complaint; and who, when that is removed, will sweep them onward with a tyranny infinitely more ruthless than any from which they have escaped. A feeling of this kind induced one of the deserters to return, and to give information that this band had formed the diabolical plan of making a night incursion, the object of which was to carry off the females of Lord —'s family. It became, therefore, proper that they should be immediately sent off the island without waiting for a better vessel than the little fishing schooner. They accordingly embarked on board of her. The first lieutenant was dispatched in this charge. Lieut. H— was put under his orders in the large cutter, to accompany him to a little settlement in New Brunswick, called Percy, near to which is a safe land-locked anchorage called Gaspee Bay. Here, it was hoped, some vessels would be found which Lieut, H— could bring back to our relief. Meantime, this bay was appointed as the place of general rendezvous.

In about ten days, Lieut. H— returned, bringing with him three fishing-schooners, which were not adequate to carry off the crew and the stores that had been saved. A part was, however, embarked on board two of them. The captain remained on the island by the wreck, and there now remained with him but a small portion of the well- affected part of the crew. We sailed in the schooners with a fair wind, and lost sight of our low-wooded island; but the wind died away soon after, and we continued for several days, with light variable winds and calms, to make but little way. On the afternoon of the third or fourth day, we descried through the haze a large ship standing towards us; she was near to us before we saw her, so that we were not long in suspense. H. M. S. ship P— came up with us, and our commanding lieutenant went on board to give an account of our circumstances. As soon as he returned, the P— made all sail in the direction of Anticosta, instead of proceeding to Quebec, whither she had been bound. We got on towards Gaspee Bay as well as the calm weather would allow us. To those who are accustomed to the luxury of a feather-bed, this slow progress may appear irksome, crowded as we were in a small fishing-schooner, and compelled to sleep on her deck; to us youngsters it was a grand holiday to be relieved from the restraints under which our duties on board the frigate had kept us. We found fishing-lines and hooks on board, and never-failing amusement in the use of them, while perfectly calm; but, to our great annoyance, we were obliged to lay them in when a light air of wind enabled our vessel to creep through the water, however slowly, in order that her progress might not be retarded by dragging them. We were not, even then, without objects of interest and amusement, in looking at the gambols of the multitude of whales which were here congregated in greater numbers than I have ever since seen; and they, also, seemed more frolicsome and playful. I could here add my testimony, if it had been requisite, to the fact of those immense animals jumping entirely out of the water; although, more generally, their unwieldy weight allowed little more than half their length to rise above the surface, on which they fell upon their broadside with a noise like thunder. The best miniature simile I could give of the sea around us at this time, would be a pool full of trout in a fine evening; when the mayfly is on the water.

I was instructed by some of the seamen who had been whalers, that the most numerous groups were the finners, or fin-backed whales, which, being less productive and more vicious, are not sought after; but there were, also, many of the kind which are sought for their oil. I believe the demon of mischief put it into our heads to fire one or two musket-balls into some of them; but these, probably, did not trouble them much, and we had no means of attacking them in any other way. The smallness of the vessel we were in might have justified a fear for her safety, if we had then known the wonderful story of the American South-sea whaler being sunk by the repeated attacks of a whale. These gambols were performed so near us, and the whales so frequently passed close to us, that the chance of our being hit was at least three to one, if they had not instinctively avoided us, which I have no doubt they did.

We now fell in with two British brigs, transports, which having landed the troops or stores they had carried out, were returning light. Our commanding officer took possession of them; we removed into them, and the schooners were sent back to the island, where their light draught of water would make them useful. Soon afterwords we arrived at Gaspee Bay, where the holiday amusements of us youngsters were changed from fishing for cod to rambling about in a wilderness of wood; with a musket over our shoulders, (for I cannot say that we found much game,) and returning on board in time for our dinner of pork and molasses. I never had an opportunity of seeing this dish at the table of an American, but the fashion of using such combination has been attributed to them; and the captain of our transport thought proper to give it to us, I suppose, upon the principle of conformity; although we were not in the United States, but in British America, where the custom does not prevail. I do not know how I might relish this mess now, but I am quite sure I found no objection to it then. Leaving the transport anchored in this nicely-sheltered bay, we may return to H. M. ship P— which had arrived at Anticosta.

The site of the mutinous deserters' haunt was supposed to be about four miles from the tents. Off this spot H. M. ship P— anchored, and sent an armed party, including the whole of her marines, to search for, and if possible, to take some of them dead or alive. The mutineers came down to the beach, also armed, with the show of an intention to repel this party; but after firing off their muskets at the boats, when they were yet for from the shore, they ran into the wood without waiting for any closer encounter, and thus only gave a more direct intimation of the place of their retreat. The party from the P— pushed into the wood; but they soon discovered that looking for their opponents in a tangled thicket of indefinite extent, would be only a waste of time. By a diligent search, however, they discovered the place in which they had deposited their stores and provisions, and also their arms; of which last they appeared to have disencumbered themselves, to make their retreat more freely. This den was, of course, cleared out, and every article taken from it on board. The P— next embarked the captain of His Majesty's late ship and the remainder of her crew, with such stores as could be got on board without loss of time; and, calling for us at Gaspee Bay, proceeded to Halifax, where the crew of the lost ship were distributed among the ships of the squadron. The captain and officers remained on board the P— for a passage to England. Before returning thither, however, it was necessary that she should fulfil the object of her voyage, by going to Quebec for a convoy; so that we found ourselves there again sooner than we expected.

The mutineers who were left to their fate upon the Island of Anticosta, probably found no difficulty in getting off in some of the many small vessels which would, after the departure of His Majesty's ship P—, come to get what they could from the wreck. The number of these deserters would give them the power, which they would no doubt use; of asserting a right of property in the wreck, and making their terms with such vessels for a passage to the United States, where they probably became afterwards available subjects. to add to the Englishmen with which the American frigates were manned.

From the account given me by many seamen, whom I have interrogated upon that subject since the conclusion of the war, I am induced to believe that the crews of those ships are in a great part made up of British men-of-war's men, and almost all their petty officers were such. The system of discipline in the American ships was quite as rigid as it was in ours, or even more so; but *they had no compulsory service, and their term of enlistment was limited.* Our seamen were invited also to desert from their unlimited and compulsory service, by the popular motto of "Free Trade and Seamen's Rights;" the pay in the American service was greater, and the limited nature of their engagement admitted of their having free liberty to roam on shore and spend their money without danger of the ships being unmanned by desertion.

These circumstances, together with the embargo on the marine commerce of America, which brought forward a thousand competitors from whom to select every hundred that was wanted for their ships, gave the Americans immense advantages ; but, notwithstanding all these, notwithstanding that they did not man their ships with Luddites and convicts, notwithstanding that they did not impress able seamen from their industrious though daring occupations to serve upon an equal footing with these convicts, still, the great advantage was in the over- whelming difference of force in vessels of the same nominal class. A book written by Mr. James[1] on this subject, very properly assigns a due consideration to weight of metal as an element in estimating the force of ships. It is one which is not in general sufficiently considered. Thus, in looking at the classing of our own ships, we speak of a thirty-two and a thirty-six gun frigate, and the difference does not seem great, but when we know that the thirty-two carried only 12-pounders, and the thirty-six carried 18-pounders, a new element enters into the proportion, and the comparison will then be between thirty-two multiplied by twelve, and thirty-six multiplied by eighteen, or about thirty-two to fifty-four. But this is not all. The more massive scantling (size of the frame-work) of the larger ship is to receive the smaller shot, to bury itself in the wood with little damage; while the larger shot, coming against the smaller frame-work, or the smaller masts, smashes every thing before it.

The detail of one of the actions during our short war with America, in which the smaller vessel was sunk by the larger, has lately been related to me by a seaman, one of the few survivors of the English brig Reindeer when she was sunk by the American ship Wasp. Accounts of the action, of course, appeared at the time; but it would not be easy to convey, in any official account, the interest which this man' narrative carries with it. I shall, therefore, give it in his own words:-

"We was cruising off Falmouth, looking for these Mericans, because we had heard that some of them were off there. Our Captain comes upon deck at break of day, and he was looking all round outside of us to seaward, because we were not far from the land, and he did not expect any thing in-shore of us;

---

[1] Perhaps "A Full and Correct Account of the Chief Naval Occurrences of the Late War Between Great Britain and the United States of America; preceded by a cursory examination of the American accounts of their naval actions fought previous to that period [...]", by William James. London: T. Egerton, 1817.

when our first lieutenant calls out to him· 'Here's a sail under the land, Sir.' So with that we puts about and stands towards her, and, presently, she seed us and stood out towards us. When we had got pretty close to her, as she was not disposed to run away, we laid our head off the land and shortened sail to let her come up with us. The first broadside we gave her choaked her rudder, so we were able to take what position we liked, and for a while we had the best on it; but our Captain thought to carry her by boarding: so we tried to board her forward by her bowsprit·but they were ready for us and skivered us like as many mice. When our Captain seed that, with fourteen wounds in himself, he ordered us to retreat, and the next' broadside she gave us after that fairly ploughed up our decks, and killed our Captain with his fifteenth wound. It was the death·warrant to the brig too·she filled so fast that there was only time to get the wounded as was likely to live out of her. Them as was mortally wounded went down in her. When the Mericans boarded us there was no officer left to give any orders but the captain's clerk, ·and only twenty·five men out of one hundred and twenty. The first man as comes up to me was one of my own towns·men from Kirkcaldy; with a cutlass over my head, says he,·' You –, what's the bearing and distance from the old wharf to Aunty Nell's?[1] Down with your arms.' With that I out with my knife and cut the belt that was round my waist with a pistol and cutlass to it. At the same time he makes a dig at one of the marines, but his lieftenant stopped him; says the lieftenant· 'Would you kill a man in cold blood when he's surrendered?' I knowed the lieftenant too·he had been a lieftenant in our service, and was broke for a drop of grog when he was second lieutenant of the Seagull his name was O'Reilly. So we laid our Captain and officers as was killed all together on the quarter deck; and before we could go into the boats with the Americans, while they were getting the wounded into the boat, we nailed a white ensign over them. Soon after we shoved off from the brig she gave a sally to starboard, and went down head foremost. The Wasp's crew was

---

[1] Aunty Nell, the hostess of a public house in Kirkcaldy,

42

350 men, ours was only 120. She had 36-pounders, ours was only 24-pounders."

Our mutinous deserters have led me into rather a long digression. I shall leave the subject for the present; but as the manner of manning our navy during the last war, has occupied my mind much, I may resume it at a future time.

While H. M. S. P— lay at Quebec, waiting for the ships she was to convoy to England, a fire broke out in the Upper Town that threatened destruction to the whole. A Lieutenant from the P— was dispatched with a party to assist in putting it out. I was attached to this party, and had thus an opportunity of marking the progress of its destructive ravages. Its progress was not only by means of contact, in the way that would happen in a town where the roofs were of tiles or slates, but the houses here being roofed_with *shingle*[1] they caught fire by the sparks falling on them. A strong breeze of wind was blowing at this time, so that the fire burst forth from place to place at considerable distances from those where it already raged. The number of houses consumed must have been great. A broad belt of the town, extending from the spot where the fire had commenced to the outskirts, in the direction of the wind, was destroyed.

One church, at a good distance from the fires already burning, was seen to smoke at its roof: a rush was made to save it. It was too late. The flames burst out and soon enveloped the whole: they were communicated to a nunnery. The broad gate which enclosed the premises was locked: the key could not be found. A moment of intense anxiety prevailed. A simultaneous rush was made by the assembled crowd; the gate gave way, and the captives were released. And now more anxious to escape from the turmoil which surrounded them, than they had ever been to explore the regions of liberty beyond their convent walls, they were led to some other retreat.

Luckily, the wind did not blow in the direction of the Lower Town, where the streets were narrow and the houses crowded together. As the evening closed in, the wind died away to a calm, and the fire, having burned to the end of the town,

---

[1] Slabs of thin wood put on in the manner of slates.

exhausted itself and went out. Having collected our seamen, we got on board about eleven o'clock at night.

The vessels which were to accompany us being now ready, we sailed for England, with ten sail under our convoy, about the beginning of September. We made our way down the river without any event, and in the gulf, again met with foggy weather, in which, however, we managed to keep clear of our friend Anticosta. It was about this time that I first witnessed that scene of overpowering anxiety·a man falling overboard, with the ship under way. We were going with all sail set in a light breeze nearly before the wind, about three, knots, when the man fell out of the mizen rigging. The helm was instantly put down, and the stern-boat cleared away, while the ship rounded to. A fog was coming on. When she shoved off, the man could still be seen. The fog closed in, and we lost sight of the man and the boat. We continued to strike upon the bell until she reappeared. The man was in her · but he was a corpse! It was singular that he had not gone down; the boat found him floating, with his shoulders out of the water and his face in it. He was taken on board, laid before the galley fire, and the usual means for restoring suspended animation were resorted to, but without effect. On the next day he was returned to the watery grave from which he had been rescued in vain; but with this gratification to the survivors, that the respect of the usual solemnities attended "the committal of his body to the deep."

I have termed the case of a man's falling overboard, one of *overpowering anxiety*. The sudden alarm while the crew are dispersed at their ordinary occupations, or perhaps amusements – the simultaneous rush – and the feeling of inability to render any direct personal assistance, tend as much as almost any case I am aware of, to produce that hurry, and those misdirected efforts, which arise from that state of things emphatically called a panic. In the instance I have narrated above, every thing was done with a proper presence of mind, even to putting a compass into the boat; but I have referred to this matter more particularly, because I have often since seen the hurry and misdirected efforts I speak of, in similar cases, and where the experience of the officer in charge should have been a security against his being taken by surprise.

The first impulse in all such cases is, naturally, a desire to stop the ship at the instant, and on the spot. I think this impulse too often gives rise to the practice of letting go the lee-braces and squaring the yards when the helm is put down. When the ship is going before the wind, as in the above case, there is nothing for it but to put the helm down, and let her round to as quickly as possible. But in all cases of a ship going with the wind anywhere upon her side, before or abaft the beam, and under circumstances in which the ship will come round, I would submit to my brother officers, that the sails ought not to be backed until they back themselves. The hands, or in a well-managed ship, the watch, should instantly be called, "About ship," and the helm at the same time be put down, sail shortened in stays, and the main-yard left square on the other tack. But there should be no letting go of the braces or bowlines, until the proper order is given for changing the arrangement of the sails. If a ship be under easy sail, or in a situation where her coming round is doubtful, there will be nothing lost by making the trial, provided she be in circumstances in which she will answer her helm readily when it is put down. If the yards be squared when she shows that she will not come round, she will not be further from the man after falling off, than she would have been if the yards had been squared without trying her.

There is no pretension to any discovery in proposing the above method in the case supposed, but I am quite sure, that those of my brother officers who join me in approving of it, will admit that they have seen instances in which it might have been practised with advantage, and was not practised, from the *hurry* to throw the sails aback. The hint may, therefore, be useful to some young officer, or to an amateur in yacht sailing.

It is, perhaps, needless to add, that, in all cases, the quick dispatch of the boat is a point of the greatest importance. I may remark, that what has been said about putting about on the other tack, in the supposed case, is more particularly applicable to fore and aft rigged vessels, from the greater facility with which it can be done.

After these observations, it can do no harm to repeat a maxim which has been suggested elsewhere, viz. that an officer should frequently, in his watch, or any other charge, exercise his mind by suggesting to himself the occurrence of the possible accidents in which he may be called upon to act promptly, and in considering what steps should be taken in them, that he may not be unprepared, but ready to suppress the alarm of those around him, and give confidence by his coolness.

CHAPTER IV

AFTER beating about the Gulf for some time, with foul winds and fogs, and being unable to round the south end of Newfoundland, we bore up to pass through the Strait of Bellisle, i.e. between Newfoundland and the coast of Labrador. In the narrowest part of this channel, there is an island called Bellisle, which gives its name to the Strait. There is a passage for ships on either side of the island, so that, in fact, the channel is, in this place, divided into two straits.

On our progress towards these narrows we had variable winds, and were often enveloped in fogs. The frequent shifting of the wind made it more troublesome for our little convoy to keep company with us at night; but when those changes were accompanied by a fog, it seemed quite beyond their powers of calculation to judge what course they should steer, or on what tack they should go, if the wind would not allow them to steer the course which had been directed by signal before the night or the fog came on. Accordingly, when they managed to get beyond the hearing of our bell or drums, the use of which respectively indicated the tack we were on, they spread abroad over the whole breadth of the channel, until a clear glimpse allowed of our calling them together again.

A rather long continuance of one of those fogs was broken up by a fine breeze from the northward, about ten in the forenoon, when we were somewhat puzzled by finding our ten sail reduced to three. As the weather became clearer, the mystery was unravelled, and we saw · our seven sail all snugly collected far from us under the land upon the Newfoundland side of the strait; but – there was an eighth sail with them! They looked like little specks in the haze of the horizon; but the lofty sails of the eighth, lightly shadowed on the dark land behind them, showed like the ghost of some giant ship. When we discovered this, we made sail towards them, and beat to quarters. The stranger stood out to meet us. She might well do so, for as she approached, we could perceive a double tier of guns, and other indications of her being a line-of-battle ship. When we had neared her a little more, another large ship was seen to follow her from under the land. It was now time to look out for the safety of His Majesty's ship.

When we had first stood towards the enemy, the remaining three vessels of our convoy had been ordered to make the best of their way in an opposite direction towards the westernmost of the two straits. We now tacked to follow them, and had not long done so, when a third large ship was seen standing out. They crowded all sail in chase, and the two leaders of the enemy were visibly gaining upon us, when, about four o'clock, it fell calm. By this time we were near to the small remainder four convoy, and the calm no longer admitted of our running away, or of the enemy pursuing, so we had a quiet time to survey each other for the rest of the afternoon. The Frenchmen hoisted their colours; and as any attempt to deceive them would have been futile, we also hoisted ours.

The night set in dark and cloudy, and before the twilight had quite gone, we lost sight of them. By eight o'clock our three little friends had contrived to close about us, like chickens round a hen when a kite is seen to hover near. By this time also it was very dark, and a fine breeze springing up, enabled us · to steer through the western strait, and to get well to the northward of the Island of Bellisle before it again fell calm.

The Frenchmen, judging by themselves, had no idea that we would persevere, after it was dark, in doing that which we had shown to be our intention while it was day. They accordingly *all* made for the eastern strait. Had they separated, they most probably would have caught us; or, at all events, would have taken the remainder of our convoy; but such were not the French naval tactics of that day in chasing a British man-of-war. As it was, the breeze which we had in the western strait, carried us well to the northward of the island, while the Frenchmen appeared to have had light winds, which had barely sufficed to carry them past the narrowest part of the eastern strait. Such was our relative position as we lay again becalmed, when the noon of the following day dispersed the fogs which intercepted our sight, and showed that we had so far the start of them.

In the afternoon, a fine breeze sprang up from the north-west, which enabled us, with our little flock, to shape a course round the north end of Newfoundland; and as we were about to lose sight of our pursuers, by bringing that land between them and us, we had the satisfaction of seeing them lie still in the mouth of the strait, in all the helplessness of a perfect calm, with their sails hanging sluggishly against the mast; so we again hoisted our colours by way of a farewell salute. Our north-wester increased to a heavy gale as we left the land; and rolling across the Atlantic under bare poles, we made the white cliffs of Old Albion with clear weather, and a fair wind up Channel brought us to an anchor in the Downs.

In all the voyages I have made since, I have never descried the cliffs of Old England without emotion. This was my first return from a foreign voyage, and my feelings on seeing the land are yet freshly alive in my mind. The buoyancy of those feelings has been surpassed only by that which accompanied an arrival in Leith Roads a year and a half afterwards, on a brief visit of a month to my friends. I may mention, by the way, that this was the only absence from service which exceeded a fortnight, during twenty-two years.

Soon after our arrival, we were despatched for some purpose to Elsineur, where we arrived about the end of December. Our stay there was not many days, but the recollection of the cold at that time enables me better to estimate Shakspeare's expression of "A nipping and an eager air," which Horatio felt when he was waiting with Hamlet for the ghost on the platform at this place; and I even now shiver at the remembrance of my two hours' spell at the mast-head on that occasion. I believe it was the last instance of my being subjected to this sort of school-boy discipline.

While we lay at Elsineur, another British man-of-war happened to be there also, whose Captain was senior to ours. It was usual for men-of-war, lying in a roadstead, to send their top-gallant yards down at sunset; and in this and many other movements which they performed simultaneously, it is not customary for any signal to be made; but, by a sharp look out on the Admiral's or senior Captain's ship, and by watching his preparations for any such movement, the other ships should be able to perform it along with him; and they frequently beat him, which is all fair, provided they do not begin before he shows them the example. As I mentioned before, the usual time for sending down top-gallant yards was sunset. I happened to be the midshipman in charge of the afternoon watch. Now, although it was very cold, yet there was a clear blue sky overhead, and the haze near the horizon did not prevent the sun from showing himself to be considerably above it. On this account I was not yet upon the look-out for the top-gallant yards, whereas I ought to have been upon the watch for every thing. It happened, however, that the commanding officer on board the senior ship, did not like the prospect of being disturbed from his dinner to send down the top-gallant .yards, and, therefore, resolved to *make it sunset* before he should go down: so, off went the muskets of the sentinels, and when I looked round, it was to see the top-gallant yards of the Commodore come trippingly down. In vain did I jump to the hatchway to give notice to the First-Lieutenant; he met me on the ladder. The orders for getting down our top-gallant yards, and maledictions on my neglect, followed in quick succession; and, as soon as they were down, I was ordered to take the place of one of them at the fore-top mast-head. This was all right so far as I was concerned, but at the time I thought it very unfair to *make it sunset* while I could see the sun, as I went aloft, still twice his own diameter above the horizon.

After narrowly escaping being frozen in, we got out of the Baltic, and in crossing the North Sea, were thrown upon our broadside during a thick snow-shower, by a violent unforeseen squall, which caught us with the top-sails at the mast-head. For some seconds it seemed uncertain whether she would recover. She balanced the right way, however, and we reached Sheerness in safety, where it was necessary for the ship to undergo some repairs. Who that has been at Sheerness in modern days, would recognise it as the same place which existed under that name in January 1797? Of all the extensive improvements which have been made, there is none greater than the removal of that nuisance which existed at the time we speak of in full perfection within the precincts of the dockyard, under the name of the *Old Ships*[1]. What officer or midshipman of that day does not remember the anxious responsibility under which he lay to prevent desertion from his boat's crew or party

---

[1] *Hulks used for housing of workers and their families, like tenements; Workers were evicted in 1802.*

of men? and who does not recollect, with horror, the facility which these *old ships* offered for this purpose. Conceive three old line-of-battle ships hauled up alongside of one another. (This, by the way, must have cost some trouble, for we had not in those days the splendid invention of *Mr. Morton's slip*.) Conceive three such ships alongside of each other, connected by gangboards through some of their port-holes, and the whole capacious space inclosed within their wooden walls, divided into cabins, opening from narrow passages, which intersected one another in all directions; and each tier, or deck, of these cabins and passages communicating by numberless trap-holes, with a ship-ladder to answer for a stair. Conceive each of these cabins to be a shop, where the sale of gin was the ostensible occupation of its inmates, which served as a cover for the nefarious and villainous practices, to which such a warren insured safety and concealment. Suppose all this, reader, and you may imagine how great a relief to the mind of a youngster in charge of a boat's crew in Sheerness Dockyard, was the destruction of the old ships; and how great was this benefit, among many others, conferred on the public by the judgment and decision of Lord St. Vincent; although even this reformation, palpable as it seems, did not escape the clamour of the day among those whose tender mercies considered the number of "poor people" who were thus deprived of their habitations. In this consideration, no account was taken of the scenes of depravity and murder which such receptacles hid from the day, while they afforded a sanctuary to the perpetrators, whom no external power could reach, as long as they kept on good terms with their brethren in iniquity. Among other malpractices, that of kidnapping seamen to make them drunk, was one. When drunk, they robbed them, if they had money, and if they had not, when poor Jack got sober, and was thoroughly afraid of returning to his ship, after an absence without leave, his *friends* did him the loving-kindness of conveying him to Blackwall, and there selling him to some Jew, who was employed as an agent for manning an Indiaman. It is not easy to imagine how such a nuisance could have been created and permitted long to exist in one of His Majesty's dockyards. The old ships were probably at first intended as habitations for the artificers of the dock- yard, but they had become such dens as I have described them.

After refitting at this sweet place (Sheerness), we were next dispatched with a convoy to see them half-way across the Atlantic, safely past the track of the enemy's privateers, which watched for the destruction of our commerce. To our great delight, we were to cruise our way back among these marauders.

Who does not recollect the elastic bound of feeling diffused among the crew, "the spring and the alacrity" shown by every man and boy on board, when the orders for such an independent cruise became known, and the ship with which they were identified was relieved from the drag of a convoy, or the still more wearing *ennui* of a blockade? In such a cruise too, there was no drawback to the most tender conscience on the subject of prize-money. No "white-handed old gentleman, calm and dignified under his calamity," deprived of his *plata*, the fruits of a long life of ease and industry. Here was all the excitement of a continued fox-chase: our field was the ocean, and our game the enemy's men-of-war and privateers. To meet with an enemy's merchant-ship on the ocean at that time, was an occurrence too rare to be looked for.

In a blockading fleet, when you first join, there is some interest for a time: while the movements of the enemy's ships have the power to make you fancy that they are about to come out. But when you become familiar with all this, when repeated disappointment deprives you of faith in those movements, when the enemy's ships become to you like so many signal-posts on the land, which it is your duty to count morning and evening,- then comes the tiresome stretch of anxiety to keep your ship clear of her neighbours in dark squally nights, with sudden shifts of wind, and to maintain her station accurately in all the monotony of a line of *close march*, night after night, day after day, and month after month. But in the delightful freedom of a cruise on the ocean, every morning brought some new source of excitement.

We escorted our convoy to the appointed limit without any event, but one of those which makes the charge of a convoy a sad abatement from the delight of such a free cruise as I have referred to. It happened that a sail was seen upon the lee-bow, the wind at N.N.W.; so we were close hauled with our convoy upon the starboard tack. The stranger was on the opposite tack standing towards us. The contrast between us and our convoy soon showed her what we were; and her tacking from us and making all sail, together with the lofty and broad spread of her canvass, showed clearly that she was one of the enemy's frigates, or one of the many frigate-built ships which the merchants of Bourdeaux had fitted out as privateers.

We made all sail in chase. In a run of three hours we fancied that we ha gained upon her a little, but we were not near enough to keep sight of her when the night should close in, and the top sails of our convoy sinking in the horizon, reminded our captain that "ships appointed for the guard or convoy of merchant ships must diligently attend upon that charge without fail, and without diverting to other posts or occasions." We were, therefore, obliged to give up the chase. She hoisted her colours to give us a salute at parting, as we had done to the enemy's three ships in the straits of Bellisle. We rejoined our convoy, and having fulfilled our duty to them, we set off in all the freedom of an unfettered cruise. We got upon the track of our homeward bound trade, and for a time saw no enemy.

On the night between the 11th and 12th of April, I had the middle watch upon deck (from twelve till four.) When was relieved and had left the deck, soon after four, there was as yet no daylight; it was a cloudy morning, and we were standing on the larboard tack under easy sail (topsails and foresails.) I was not long in taking off my jacket and trowsers, stowing them in the clew of my hammock, and fixing my shoes and cap there also to be ready for a start: in two minutes I should have been in a most luxurious slumber. I heard some stir upon deck, and a voice calling down the main hatchway – "Drummer, beat to quarters !" The care in stowing away my clothes was rewarded by the readiness with which I found them. Before the drummer bent to quarters I had time to go on the weather gangway and see the cause of the movement.

A large ship had crossed a-head of us on the opposite tack. Our guns might possibly have reached her, but she was too far forward on the bow for them to bear upon her, and she was now in the act of going about, so that she stood upon the same tack as ourselves, and upon our weather-bow. We got into her wake; but, although we had thus gained to windward a little, in keeping a more full sail she had drawn from us. When daylight dawned she was still sufficiently on our bow to show a broad yellow streak studded with thirteen guns, the same number which one side of our own main-deck battery presented. She hoisted the tricoloured flag of the French Republic. It soon became evident that going to windward was not the Frenchman's point of sailing. He seemed sensible of this, and continued to edge away half a point at a time, till we had him nearly before the wind. There was a moderate breeze from the N.E. and no friendly port between him and the West Indies. The equality of sailing almost justified the idea of the chase being continued over the three thousand miles of ocean that intervened. Nothing seemed to be gained on either side. The guns were kept ready primed; the topsail yards were slung, topsail sheets stoppered, and lower yards slung in the top chains. There was nothing now to be done; breakfast-time came, and now appeared the comforts of a frigate over a line-of-battle ship. On the lower-gun deck of a line-of-battle ship, where the people mess, all their goods and chattels must have been cleared away, and in such a case many of them thrown overboard; but by there being no guns on the lower-deck of a frigate, the people's mess-berths remain undisturbed in action, unless it be by a chance shot finding its way among their bowls and platters.. Our men had time to get their breakfasts in peace, and give many an opinion and crack many a joke about *the prize.*

The time came for them to be called up again, but there was nothing to do. Jack does not like to be idle; at least, he likes to be doing something: the frolic now was to propitiate the female figure-head of our good frigate, to make her go along. For this purpose, the sailors quartered on the forecastle, and some others that stole up from their quarters on the main-deck to see what was going on, began to ornament her. She was accordingly gaily bedizened, and one funny fellow, taking care that she should not want for breakfast, supplied her with a biscuit and a pot of beer. But all would not do – there she remained stretching her arms towards the Frenchman with his broad tricolour flag flying, and each ship retaining precisely the same position to the other. In a chase of five days we were never two gun-shots asunder. Of course we lay at quarters all the time.

By the third day the sameness of the scene began to be wearisome. Towards noon the look-out-man at the mast-head called out – "A strange sail on the larboard bow." We were steering about S.W. and we soon discovered her from the deck, bearing south: a ship-of-war standing to the northward on the starboard tack so as to cut us off. By way of a hint of encouragement to the crew, our captain said aloud to the first-lieutenant, "if this is another Frenchman we'll stand by to board the largest and turn her guns upon the other." A very good intention - but it was superseded by the stranger making the private signals, and turning out to be His Britannic Majesty's ship F—. She joined us in the chase, which made our friend, the prize, alter his course to the westward. The F— was commanded by a captain junior to ours, so that we played the part of commodore, and made signals, &c.

About three o'clock it became calm. The launch, or largest boat of a man-of-war, has the means of mounting a carronade, so that she may he used as a kind of gun-boat. Our launch was ordered to be prepared, and a signal was made to the F— to send her launch on board of us so armed. Our captain's notion was a very good one. He thought that the boats might cripple the Frenchman's rigging, without running any greater hazard of being sunk than such a risk as is necessarily attendant on any enterprize of "pith and moment." On the other hand, there was to be considered the delay which might arise from having to hoist the launches in, or tow them in case of a breeze springing up. Now, if I were engaged in the delightful freedom of writing a fiction, I might despatch the boats, make a very gallant attack, knock away the Frenchman's topmasts, &c., but as I am not soaring into the regions of fancy, I must disappoint my readers, and inform them, that instead of our signal being duly answered by the F— we were astonished by a signal for our captain to repair on board of her, and at the same time an admiral's flag was displayed from her mizen-top-gallant-mast-head. Rear-Admiral W— was on board, on his passage home from a command in the Mediterranean. The Admiral did not approve, and thus an end was put to the scheme of the launches.

A breeze again sprang up, and the chase continued. Towards the close of the following day the weather became more unsettled, and during the night we had frequent spirts of wind and showers, that made us stand by our lofty sails and sometimes lose sight of the chase. About two in the morning we had rather a sharp, bleak squall, attended with a change of wind, and rain that obscured our view for some time. The change of wind enabled the Frenchman to haul up, which he did, with a view of passing between his pursuers, and thus to attempt making off in a direction opposite to that in which he had been going. The darkness, for a time, favoured his manoeuvre; but in the end he made a dead failure. When the squall cleared off he was nearer to both the ships than he had been before, particularly to the F—. Another squall brought her near enough to send a few shot over and about him,[1] when he immediately struck without even firing a gun – "*pour l'honneur du pavillon.*"

The boats from both the ships were employed to remove the prisoners, who were about 250 in number, rather more than the crew of H. M. S. P—, and in all respects the two ships were so well matched that it was a pity the matter bad not been decided in a fair battle.

The merchants of Bourdeaux, who had fitted out L'Incroyable, had, no doubt, anticipated a golden harvest – at all events, they had sown most liberally for it. In all respects her men, arms, and equipments placed her on the footing of a two-and-thirty gun frigate. But in thus showing her force to be equal to that of the P—, we must not attribute blame too hastily to her commander for endeavouring to avoid an action with her, whatever we may do for his tame surrender without an effort, for he ought to have taken the chance of knocking away some of the spars of his assailants. But in trying to get

---

[1] The terms *he* and *she* have both been used in speaking of the chase. This is quite usual in sea phraseology, *she* refers directly to the *ship* – but in speaking of the motions which imply design, the ship, or the person conducting her, may be spoken of indiscriminately.

off from the P— he did no more than an English privateer would probably have done in the same circumstances. In licensing such a vessel, the object which the Government have in view is to annoy the commerce of the enemy; and that which the merchants aim at in fitting her out is to enrich themselves. Thus, whatever may happen in cases where spirited commanders of such ships are led by their own feelings, the object of privateers is not to seek an action for the support of national honour, or even the protection of national commerce. At a time when the commerce of France made it profitable for English merchants to fit out such vessels, we have heard of some instances in which so good an understanding subsisted between them and French ships of the same description, that they not only did not fight when they met, but were most friendly auxiliaries in the way of helping each other to useful information.

The merchants of Bourdeaux, as well as providing every article which was requisite in furnishing their ship with the sinews of war, were no less liberal in supplying the desideratum of Captain Dougal Dalgetty, and I am quite sure, that if the stomach of that redoubted commander could have stood the tumbling and tossing, even he would have been satisfied with the provent on board of her, and would have been a competitor for the honour of assisting to carry her into port. I was one of the happy few selected for this purpose. A lieutenant from the F—commanded her, and two midshipmen from each of the ships were his officers. The French Commissary and Doctor were allowed to remain on board the prize, and under their management the cabin fare was provided in that ample way which bespoke their desire to leave behind them as few of the good things as possible, when they should go to all the discomfort and meagre provision of a French prison in England. Accordingly the table groaned with turkeys, hams, &c. and our dessert every day displayed all the variety of dried and preserved fruits and other *bonsbons*, in the preparation of which the French are so ingenious, and for which their climate furnishes such ample means.

We were seated at the breakfast-table on a calm morning, chatting over the remains of a luxurious breakfast, when the midshipman on deck informed the lieutenant that a boat from one of the frigates was coming on board; soon afterwards two French officers came into the cabin. The *Docteur* and the Commissaire started from their seats and flew into the arms of the strangers, when a scene of such kissing took place as could only be outdone by the meeting of parted lovers. Having had a night-watch, I had not yet been upon deck since daylight, so on witnessing these embraces, my first fancy was, that one of the frigates had taken another prize, and that these new comers were, at least, the sons or brothers of our friends; but no-they were only their messmates, who had been separated from them two days! After the kissing was over, we had a little crying and lamentation, until one of them pronounced the magic words of – "*Fortune de la Guerre!*" "*Fortune de la Guerre!*" was echoed by each, their elasticity of spirit recovered its spring, and all was *gaieté de coeur.*[1]

---

[1] *Extract from a letter to the Admiralty from the Hon. William Waldegrave, vice-admiral of the Blue, to Mr. Nepean, dated on board His Majesty's Ship Flora, at Spithead, the 24th of April, 1797.*

"I beg that you will please inform the Lords Commissioners of the Admiralty that I sailed from Lisbon, with my flag on board His Majesty's Ship Flora, Captain Middleton Commander, on the 3d of this month, and arrived this day at Spithead, in company with the Pearl Frigate. On the 12th instant I fell in with the above Frigate, lat. 43 deg. 48 min. North; Long. 13 deg. 11 min. West, she being then in chace of a French Privateer; we instantly joined in the chace, which compelled the enemy to haul her wind, not withstanding which, it was not until the 13th, at 3 quarters past 11 P.M. that we found ourselves close alongside of her, and even this was owing to the Privateer's being becalmed, and our carrying the breeze up with us. On the first broadside she struck. She is called L'Incroyable, mounts 24 guns on her main deck and had on board 220 men. She belonged to Bordeaux, and sailed from that port on the 2d instant. She fortunately had made no capture, though reputed to be the fastest sailing vessel from France. I was informed by Captain Ballard that he had been in chace of her from the morning of the 11th."

CHAPTER V

THE late officers of L'Incroyable, now prisoners on board the frigates, although treated with every hospitality, soon began to feel the want of those luxuries which had been so fully supplied to them by their liberal employers. In vain was the single roast fowl presented for a *bonne-bouche*, after the pea-soup and salt-pork had gone their round, and been relieved by a dish of salt-fish at the bottom, and a sea-pie at the head, in which the King's Own served a more substantial purpose than merely to flavour it. The Frenchmen dropped some sarcastic remarks upon English good living, and began to talk about the dainties they had left behind. Their entertainers thought it a pity that they should not be allowed to share them, and upon these very considerate views being represented to the Captain of one of the frigates, he permitted a boat to be sent on board for some of the good things. The boat was liberally supplied with kegs, which contained each a turkey, a goose, or a nice round of spiced beef. The kegs were filled up with lard, which excluded the external air, and preserved the valuables within; but their contents were certainly not equal in flavour to poultry that had not undergone this mode of preservation. To the difference of our palates, now so much pampered, we had become sensible; for we had abundant opportunities of comparing them with the produce of the poultry-coops, which was also in excellent condition. When the boat had been laden with the above articles, together with cases of dried and preserved fruits, we heard some sinister observations about the abundance of the live-stock, and the account given by the Frenchmen on board the frigate of their thriving state. The boat, however, being pretty well filled, shoved off with what she had got; and, as the breeze was now springing up, we hoped that we should make sail without being favoured with another visit. But we were not to be let off so easily. As soon as she was cleared, she returned with a message, intimating that a portion of the live-stock was to be sent. A cackling, henceforth, commenced among the hen-coops, which were robbed of nearly half their inmates.

When the ambassador employed on this mission came to the turkey- coops, he exclaimed in a tone of disappointment-"

Here are but two! you have not eaten seven already? The Frenchmen tell us they left nine."

The Lieutenant commanding said, "There certainly were more in the morning. Send for Jean, le Poulailler." (*Jemmy Ducks,* we should have called him.) Our commanding officer was not yet acquainted with the joke that was in progress, but the youngsters knew very well that he would have no objection to it. Jean, le Poulailler, who had been retained in his former station under the new regime, understood what was going on, and shrugging up his shoulders, pronounced – "*En voila tous.*" "I declare," says a midshipman of the boat, who had been in her in her former trip, " I thought I had counted seven." "Oh!" replied his compatriot of the opposite interest, "they had their feathers spread out, man." "Perhaps they had," said the other, who thus allowed himself to be persuaded out of the evidence of his senses. The boat shoved off, and returned to the frigate. She was hoisted up, and we all made sail.

When every thing was quiet and in order, the ingenious young gentleman who had accounted for the numerous appearance of the turkeys by the spread of their feathers, stepped over from the leeside of the quarter-deck, and touching his hat as he passed the Lieutenant to windward, said, "It is time to give the turkeys a little air again, Sir." And going up to a colour-chest, which stood abaft the mizen-mast, and which had been emptied of its flags for the occasion, opened the lid, while the French Jemmy Ducks took out five glorious fat turkeys, and restored them to their wonted habitation.

In due time we arrived at Spithead, and as the F— had come from the Mediterranean, we were all put in quarantine. Two persons came on board to see that the quarantine laws were duly observed, and to supervise the smoking of letters previous to their being handed into the boats, by means of a long rod slit at the end. When these grave and consequential persons came on board, they told us that there had been some *disturbance* in the fleet, but that it was all now settled. This was soon after the 23rd of April, on which day Lord Bridport had resumed the command of the grand fleet, with authority from the Admiralty to say, that the complaints contained in the petition of the seamen should be redressed.

Bad as the treatment of the seamen had been, it seems probable that their mutinous combination which presented this petition, would never have been organized, had it not been through the instrumentality of some of the disaffected on the land. At all events, the delegates had their correspondents on shore after the mutiny had broken out. But it is a curious fact, that these incendiaries on the land had no power to excite the men who took upon themselves the direction of this mutiny, farther than to secure the objects which their *first* petition embodied; and that the men did not allow themselves to be led to make innovations or amplifications upon this, their first petition, when they ascertained their power, on seeing the concession of the Government after it was awakened to look at the urgency of the case by a second refusal of the fleet to put to sea. This concession was as complete as the tardiness to resolve whether it should be made or not seems unaccountable. The first act of decided and general mutiny was on the 14th of April, after several anonymous letters had been written by the men to Lord Howe, whom they styled "The seaman's friend," knowing that his Lordship affected that character; but naval officers of that day thought that he did so invidiously in reference to them.

On that day the signal was made to weigh. The men of the fleet, instead of repairing to their respective stations, simultaneously ran up the rigging and gave three cheers to show their unanimity. In this general act of insubordination the marines were included, which rendered any effort of the officers to put it down by physical force so hopeless, that it was not attempted. These circumstances would seem to have been sufficiently imperious to call for a prompt decision on the part of the Government. Upon the 23rd of April, when the seamen had the promise of redress and pardon through Lord Bridport, they returned to their duty; but though the men again obeyed the command of their officers, the organized combination was kept up among them, which watched with jealousy the tardiness that still delayed the passing of an act for this redress into a law. A resolution not to go to sea until it should be so passed, "unless the enemy was known to be at sea," was also persevered in. This gave the disaffected persons on shore a farther opportunity of exciting discontent,

Upon the authority of a man who was afterwards a messmate with me as purser, but who was then before the mast in one of the mutinous ships, this discontent was much inflamed at a meeting of the delegates, by the following address from one of the leaders. "You have been told that your petition was laid on the table-but it's all a d··d lie — it was thrown under the table, as this letter will let you know; and the writer of this letter saw it done."

The principal grievances contained in the petition of the seamen were two. First, that their pay had not been raised since the reign of Queen Anne, "at which time the value of money was much greater than at present." Second, that their provisions were supplied to them by the Purser's pound, and not by an honest pound.

It will be necessary to explain to a landsman, or even to some sailors of the present day, what was meant by the purser's pound. In all articles of provision liable to lose weight or measure by keeping, the purser was required to issue to the men only seven eighths of that with which he had been supplied by Government. For this purpose, his weights and measures were only seven eighths of the standard weight or measure, and were technically known by the name of purser's pound, &c. If all or any part of the other eighth remained when the annual survey was taken upon the stores in the purser's care, he took it on charge as a new supply, and was allowed a fixed price for it by the Government. Since that time, the matter is managed by a proportionate weight or measure being supplied to the purser in addition to what he is required to issue, so that Jack gets an honest pound. Thus the purser gets eight pounds of bread, out of which he serves the weekly allowance of seven pounds.

Besides this scraping of the *purser's eighth* off the sailor's allowance, there was frequently much to make him discontented with the quality of the provisions. The scrutiny of public opinion, and the industrious spirit of Lord St. Vincent had not, as yet, forced upon the Government the necessity of stopping with a strong hand the abuses of jobbers and contractors; so that, although the best of every thing was paid for by the country, the supplies of provisions were often of an inferior quality. Where complaints were made, the rules of the service then, as now, enjoined superior or commanding officers "to cause such present remedy to be had," as the case might require; but this present remedy was only within the immediate power of the superior officer, when the articles complained of were absolutely "rotten, stinking, and unfit for men to eat."

It must be considered, also, that the greatest portion of these mutineers had been placed where they were by a power unknown to, and at variance with, the laws of their country; and when thus made outlaws without a crime, they were retained there by fear of the most severe coercion alone. It is not, then, to be wondered at that they were disposed to look upon the officers who were made the instruments of thus retaining them, with jealousy and distrust; and to nurse feelings of rancour and discontent even when they had a ground of complaint that lay within the power of their officers to cure, rather than to run the risk of their complaint being construed into that disposition to rebel, which they were too conscious of feeling. Also, where a system of injustice was at all events to be supported, the officer whose duty it became to support such a system, was, it must be confessed, placed in circumstances which inclined him to watch with jealousy any disposition in the men to make complaints, so that the poor devil who was able to put his words into intelligible form, and was so unguarded as to become spokesman, was too often set down as a sea-lawyer, and in that character was sure of a dozen or two in addition to what he might have otherwise got when he fell into any scrape.

Thus, the situation of the seamen on board a man-of-war, which has been so much ameliorated since that time, had been neglected until it had arrived at a climax of misrule as great as the spirit of Britons could bear; and it is no wonder that the mutiny broke out. If the business-like power which produced the systematic and extensive organization of this mutiny surprises us when we consider what the men were who directed it, we ought, under all the circumstances, to be still more disposed to admire their moderation and firmness in stopping it where they did.

The name of the leading delegate, whom all seemed to follow, was Joyce. The conduct of this man in ruling, restraining, and stopping this mutiny, showed him to be possessed of that master-spirit under which mankind willingly and instinctively place themselves when engaged in dangerous enterprises. If we must lament that he was induced by any circumstances to take the lead in a measure so full of danger to his country, we cannot but admire the singular accuracy with which he estimated his power of preventing its being carried further, and the good faith with which he exercised that influence. I believe this instance of accurate calculation upon such a question by the leaders of rebellion, is a solitary one in their history. Parker declared at his trial, and continued to maintain till his death, that he had nothing to do with the planning of the mutiny at the Nore, and that in its progress, he prevented excesses which the men would have committed. This might be true, but the spirit of Joyce was capable of controlling the turbulent spirits of which he had usurped the direction, with a hand so dexterous, that they were not allowed to feel that the reins of discipline had been loosened in the change, and prevented those he led from going beyond the point he had fixed for them.

To discover what has been this man's progress in after life, would be an interesting subject of inquiry, and it would be an amusing speculation to consider what it might have been if he had had such a field as France was at that time, open before him, and if he had possessed the selfishness of a Buonaparte.[1]

Leaving our prize safe in Portsmouth Harbour, we returned from being officers and faring sumptuously every day, to our more humble station and homely fare of the Midshipman's berth on board the P—, and were so busily

---

[1] *From the website ageofsail.wordpress.com: "Records of the time being what they are, it is difficult to trace and explain Joyce's career after the mutiny. It looks as though he was admitted to the hospital at Haslar in 1798 and joins the bomb ketch Vesuvius as an Able Seaman and is quickly rated quartermaster's mate and then midshipman. Vesuvius paid off in November 1799 and Midshipman Joyce went to the 18-gun brig Brazen. On January 25, 1800 the Brazen was driven by a gale onto the Ave Rocks under Newhaven Cliffs, [...], Sussex and all but one sailor drowned."*

engaged in preparing to get to sea again, that we worked even on Sunday.

I think it was on Sunday, the 7th of May, that I was employed with a party of hands at the fore-hatchway, getting up empty water casks, when a rattling of musketry was heard not far from us. My men did not ask leave to go and see what it was, but instantly, with every man and boy in the ship, made a rush to the larboard-gangway to gaze on His Majesty's Ship London, on board of which the firing was. It did not last long; all was again quiet. By and by a boat with some wounded men, rowed towards the shore, close under our stern; and soon afterwards a general communication by boats took place through the fleet; each ship sending her two delegates, who, with Joyce at their head, thus visited all the ships of the fleet in succession. On this day (the 7th of May), the fleet had been again ordered to put to sea, and the order was answered by the men, seamen, and marines taking possession of the fore part of the ships, and some of them pointing the guns aft. On board the London, which bore the flag of Admiral Colpoys, the disposition to act in this manner had been foreseen, and an ineffectual attempt was made to guard against it by drawing up the marines on the quarter-deck armed; the officers being also armed. The marines started from their ranks one after another, and ran forward to join the seamen on the forecastle. The first who did so was instantly shot by Lieut. Bover[1], the Second-Lieutenant. The straggling discharge of fire-arms which I have mentioned, now took place; but as the marines had deserted their post, it could not last; the officers were soon overpowered.

In the first moment of their success, the men tumultuously called for vengeance on the head of Mr. Bover. He was carried to the forecastle; the yard-ropes, which had been rove on the 23rd of April, were soon rove again, and one was applied to instant use. The noose was put round the neck of Mr. Bover. Up to this point, the mutineers had acted promptly towards their avowed purpose; but here there seemed a hesitation, some want of a real determination to do that which had been so clamorously called for.

---

[1] *Peter Bover. Other references identify him as first-lieutenant.*

There was a deficiency of alertness in manning the yard-rope, which, if it had been pulled upon, would have swung Mr. Bover to the fore-yard-arm. And now stepped forward one of those characters, which I trust are not yet rare in the navy, and of which the author of "The King's Own" has drawn so fine a picture in old William Adams. This old seaman, whose name I am sorry to have forgotten, stepping quietly up to one of the forecastle guns, took up the handspike belonging to it, and placing himself beside Mr. Bover, threw the noose off his neck, and declared that any man who would lay hands upon Mr. Bover, must first hang him. The boldness of this step commanded the attention of those about him, whom he now addressed in a short harangue. He told them that he bad long known Mr. Bover for a good officer in another ship before he came into the London, and that he had. done no more than every officer and man ought to do, which was to obey orders and do his duty. This address procured the instant release of Mr. Bover, but the auditors did not perceive that the reasoning in it applied equally to the Admiral in his endeavour to stop a rising mutiny. The clamour now prevailed against him but the leaders had by this time had leisure to consider the desperate circumstances in which they would be placed by any sacrifice of their officers in cold blood. They accordingly stilled the voices of the clamorous, by declaring that the Admiral should be tried by a *court-martial.* In the mean time he was placed in confinement. A meeting of the delegates, who called themselves a court-martial, took place afterwards (I think upon the Tuesday). They acquitted the Admiral on the same grounds on which the old seaman had saved the life of Mr. Bover, namely, that he had only done his duty.

Meantime each ship hoisted a red flag, and following the example of the London, each rove her yard-ropes, to show the fate that was prepared for those who should desert the cause in which they were engaged. Their crews also mounted the rigging morning and evening, and gave three cheers to attest their unanimity. Joyce, attended by the delegates in a body, visited the ships daily, to see that the regulations which he had enjoined were complied with. In conformity with the circumstances of men who had still a negociation open with the

Government, those regulations enjoined, amongst other matters, a strict care of the stores and provisions; and the floggings that were inflicted for any breach of them, were said to be severe in some of the ships. The yard-ropes at the fore-yard-arms were not applied to the extreme purpose of hanging any one by the neck, but they were repeatedly used to duck some unhappy culprit. The system by which the new regulations were enforced, as it seems to have been carried on with more judgment, so its punishments were less frequent and vigorous than those at the Nore. In this case, also, there was not time for the rigour of the system to open the eyes of the men to the nature of the desperate scrape they had got into, and to create that disgust to their leaders, which made one ship after another at the Nore desert them, and return to the command of the officers. But even during the short time that the mutiny at Spithead lasted, the regulations which were instituted, and the manner in which they were enforced, showed that whatever else might be deficient, there was no want of energy in their discipline.

While these things were going on, we remained in H. M. Ship P—, in a state of great tranquility. Not being a line-of-battle ship, nor belonging to the grand fleet, we had been neglected, and had not as yet had any visit from the delegates, nor had any of our men attempted to visit them. But at the time of cheering, the men came aft in a body. Their spokesmen took their hats off, and respectfully represented to the Captain, that they had no complaints to make, but they did not wish to be marked as being in opposition to thirty sail-of-the-line. They then mounted the rigging, and cheered with the rest of the fleet, but, as yet, they did not adopt the ensigns of mutiny by reeving the yard-ropes and hoisting the red flag.

This state of things continued on board the P— until Tuesday, when, about noon, the fleet of boats was observed to row towards her. The moment this was known, not a man or boy remained below. They were mounted on the booms, gangway, and forecastle. I think our Captain remained upon the quarter-deck, far aft, near the taf-rail: the other officers were on the quarter-deck, well aft also, so that they were not in the way of requiring any respect from our unwelcome visitors, or of the omission of it being marked to them. The youngsters, of course, pushed themselves as near to the gangway as they could, to see what was going on. None of the men were on the quarter-deck, but all before the main-mast, as I have mentioned.

Every one who has been on board a frigate, or a two-decker, will remember that the entrance to the ship from without, by the steps up the side, is quite at the after end of the gangway, and therefore, although not on the quarter-deck, is so near to it, that if any one on entering the ship shall turn his face aft, he will feel himself called upon to make the usual obeisance to this respected spot, at least if time and practice have drilled him into proper naval feeling. On the contrary, if men coming out of boats shall turn to go forward, as they do not come on the quarter-deck, this reverence may be dispensed with.

There were, therefore, three ways in which Joyce and his associates might have entered the ship. First, they might have turned towards the quarter-deck without any mark of respect which would have been positive disrespect. Second, they might have turned towards it, and having lifted their hats, proceeded to their business on the fore- castle; but they did neither. Joyce and three others, as they stepped on board, turned directly to the place where their business lay, and walked along the larboard gangway to the forecastle. They were dressed in a seaman's working dress; their canvass trowsers were clean, though marked with tar that would not wash out, and they had on clean shirts, but not their Sunday jackets or trowsers. They had no trouble in assembling the hands around them. The men crowded about them. The youngsters did not go so far as to do this, and, probably, would not have been allowed; so we did not hear the harangue. It occupied but a short time; not more than five minutes. The delegates then returned to their boats in the same order as they came on board; and still without noticing the quarter-deck, or the officers on it, who, as I have mentioned, were so far removed from the fore part of it, as to be out of the reach of this want of deference.

I have said that not more than three or four of those delegates came on board; the rest remained in the fleet of boats, which covered the water to a considerable extent on the larboard side of the ship, and lay upon their oars.

We learned afterwards that the business of these leaders of the mutiny, on board of us, had been to get two delegates appointed to join them. The first persons fixed upon for this office were the captains of the forecastle of the two watches, starboard and larboard. They were chosen *ex-officio*, as the two prime seamen of the ship, rather than from any forwardness in themselves to act in such a station. One of them was a man upwards of forty, which was a time of life that, when attained in the privations, excesses, and rough wear of a sailor before the mast, gave many of the marks, and commanded some of the veneration of old age. I forget what this man's surname was, but that is of less consequence, as he was well known by the title of Old Geordie. Old Geordie joined the stream in surrounding the delegates upon the forecastle, until he heard himself called upon to become one of them; when he very coolly made answer to the usurpers of authority.·" I 'll be —ed if I'll have anything to do with you." The dryness of this reply produced an involuntary laugh, even among those to whom it was addressed; but as they insisted upon two being nominated, the other captain of the forecastle, Robert Dryburgh, and Alexander Skene, the captain of the maintop, were fixed upon. The judgment in this selection was consistent with the other means by which the degree of order that was preserved in the fleet during the reign of this anomalous power was maintained. These two men were prime seamen, men of orderly habits, and, as the sailors say, they had never been upon the quarter-deck, meaning, that they had never been called there to answer for any bad or questionable conduct. They were both Scotchmen.

When the boats were gone, our two delegates came aft, and taking their hats off to the captain, told him of the directions they had received from their new superiors, namely, to possess themselves of the officers' arms, to remove all small arms from the after-part of the ship, and to conform to the motions of the fleet in hoisting the red flag and reeving the yard-ropes; also, that they might send on shore such officers as they did not like. They added, that they had no complaint to make of their officers, but repeated the remark, that they could not stand out against thirty sail-of-the-line. The captain sent for his servant, and directed him to give up the arms in the cabin: of course the officers followed his example. But this instruction of the leaders was not carried to the extent of preventing the officers from wearing their side-arms as a part of their uniform when they went out of the ship. When these men had stated what instructions they were to follow, our captain said · "Well, I suppose you will give me a boat to go on shore." The boat was instantly manned, and the side attended in the usual manner. Before he went in her, however, he descended to the cabin, and stopping there a short time, came upon deck again with a written paper in his hand, and ordered the crew to be called aft. They came as readily as if there had been no interruption to the routine of obedience, and he addressed them in a short speech, referring to their duty to their country, and the advantage that the French would take if the conduct of the fleet was persevered in. The speech was quite in general terms, and it had the disadvantage of being read and not spoken. It commanded silence and attention however, and when finished, the paper which contained it was thrown amongst the men, who made a scramble for the possession of it. Our captain then went on shore. The situation of the officers and men who remained on board was not an agreeable one. We continued in charge of the after-part of the ship, the forepart of which was in possession of a crew in open mutiny, and yet the business of preparing the ship for sea and receiving supplies of water and provisions went on in some degree under the direction of the proper officers, who were *consulted* about those matters. In such a disjointed state of things the equipment could not proceed rapidly · still it went on. Demands had been made for supplies of stores (rope, canvass, &c.) from the dockyard.

It was not the invariable custom then, as it has been since, for such stores to be delivered to the warrant officer, to whose department they belonged, in the presence of a commissioned officer only, but the warrant officer drew them himself, and the boat in which they were brought off was frequently under the charge of a midshipman, some-times a mere boy. I was sent on this duty by the senior lieutenant. and the boat of which I thus had the charge was manned and permitted to go by the will of the crew.

CHAPTER VI

DURING my absence from the ship an incident occurred which confirms me in the recollection that the officers were permitted to carry their side-arms when they went on shore, and that on this occasion I had on the little dirk which formed part of a midshipman's uniform. We had got the stores into the boat, and when I directed the crew, who were placed thus questionably under my command, to come into her that we might go on board, one of them told the rest that they may follow that cheese-toaster (meaning my dirk) if they liked, but he was not disposed to go off yet. However, the rest were disposed, and my independent gentleman came with us. As we rowed down the harbour on our way back to the ship, this man seemed but ill reconciled to his disappointment, and I could not help feeling some anxiety to get fairly out of the harbour, and past *the Point.* As we approached this scene of fiddling, fighting, and drinking, my trouble-some friend proposed that they should go on shore to have a glass of grog. I knew very well what the consequences would be if they went on shore at this place, so I set strenuously to work, and used all my rhetoric to prevent it, and seizing hold of the tiller, gave the boat a broad yard out from that side of the harbour. I was joined in my views by some of the more considerate, and while the matter was under discussion a strong ebb tide swept us past the Point, so that we could not easily have regained it, and we proceeded on board. Had we landed at the Point, besides the unpleasant and solitary charge of the boat and stores, that would have devolved upon me for an indefinite number of hours, among many boats' crews more mutinous than my own, and who knew me only by my midshipman's jacket and *"cheese-toaster,"* which would have been no recommendation to them, I foresaw also the predicament of going off to the ship with a part only of my boat's crew, and they in a state of drunkenness. Such conduct would have been visited with severe chastisement by the ringleaders of the mutiny if I had complained of it; but besides that this would have been no satisfaction to me, an appeal to them was of course out of the question.

This state of things had continued some days, during which our delegates attended the meetings, when they began to exercise the power they possessed, and one man who had been guilty of some very bad conduct was severely punished by being flogged, and ducked from the fore-yard-arm. The fellow's punishment was just enough, but such a measure, adopted without any appeal to the officers, brought a very unpleasant conviction of their situation.

The crew, who had at first declared that they had no complaint to make of their officers, now discovered that they did not like the surgeon, the boatswain, the chief-master's-mate (day-mate as he is called from not keeping a watch). Although this officer has no night-watch to keep, he is expected to be on the alert at all times, night and day, when any thing of consequence is going on. He is the chief assistant of the first lieutenant in stationing the men at their various duties, and in regulating the order and cleanliness of the ship in all parts below the deck. The enforcing of these duties often brings him into collision with the men, and requires a shrewdness and promptitude that is not always accompanied with that cheerfulness and good temper which are requisite to render such an officer agreeable to them. The same may be said of the boatswain. What their objection to the surgeon was, I do not know. However, these officers were told that they could not be allowed to remain in the ship any longer. A boat was manned for them, and they were landed at Point Beach, with their chests and bedding. Another instance occurred of the men taking the law into their own hands in a case that was more offensive to the feelings of the officers than the former, but they could not prevent it.

The doctor's loblolly-boy fell under their displeasure: this personage (I speak of the year 1797) was generally some poor helpless sort of creature; not often a boy, as the name imports. His business was to spread plasters, to ring the bell for patients to come to the surgeon, and to do all the drudgery of waiting on the sick in the capacity of scullion. Evan Hughes was rather a superior sort of person in this station; tidy in his dress and respectable in his demeanour, he united to the above occupations that of waiting upon the doctor as his servant — I beg pardon of the College of Physicians, but I like to retain old names; our surgeon used to be so called : neither had we any assistant-surgeons in those days – but doctor's mates. The intention, then, of the men to turn the doctor out of the ship, was known to the officers before it had been announced, and Evan Hughes was suspected of the heinous offence of betraying the secrets of the mutineers. What the amount of evidence against him was, I never heard, but they deemed it sufficient to inflict upon him the severe punishment of ducking from the foreyard-arm. When poor Evan was warned of his danger, by some expressions towards him of this sinister purpose, in vain did he run to the midshipman's berth for sanctuary. To receive him and stow him under the table was the first proposal, but it was soon recollected that he must have been seen to come in, and that the midshipmen's berth would be considered as open to search by the men in their present circumstances. One youngster thought of stowing him in his chest, but, besides that it was hardly big enough, it was outside of the berth, and the operation could not fail to be observed. It was at last decided that he should go to his late master's cabin, which opened from within the gun-room (the mess-room of the officers). To this place he found his way, but was soon made sensible that there was no security for him even here, by the parley which he overheard between the sentinel at the gun-room door and his ruthless pursuers, of whom six or eight had been despatched to bring him on the forecastle. As in the case of a machine, which will continue its motion for a time after the moving power has been taken off, so the routine of cleaning the ship, and some other matters that did not interfere with the mutiny, went on, and among them that of *planting* the sentinels at their accustomed posts with the usual orders. The sentinel at the gun-room door had orders to keep his post clear, and to prevent intrusion into the gun-room. I wish I could say, for the honour of the marine corps of that day, that any spirited attempt was made to enforce that order in the present instance; but I must not. Evan Hughes was dragged from his hiding-place, and brought on the forecastle before the assembled crew, who were to be his accusers, judge, jury, and executioners.

The yard-rope rove in a block, or pulley, at the foreyard-arm, was led through one at the mast-head, and from thence by one at the foot of the mast was laid along the deck, so that a number of men could take hold and pull upon it while they walked or ran along. From the pulley at the yard-arm the other end of this rope came down to a platform fastened at the cat-head (the projecting beam to which the anchor is attached when not in use). This, so far, is the same preparation as that made for hanging a criminal: The outer end of the rope, which was thus brought to the cat-head, instead of being applied to the neck of the victim, had, in this case, an iron crow-bar fastened to it by the middle, which, lying across the direction of the rope, formed an uneasy seat, upon which the subject of this severe discipline was placed. The rope from the crow-bar passed up between his legs, and his hands were tied to it above his head. A little above the place where his hands were fastened there was attached a toggle, or small piece of wood, the use of which was to prevent the rope from passing so far through the pulley at the yard-arm as to bring his hands in contact with it. At a given signal the men stationed to take hold of the inner end of the rope ran away with it, and poor Evan Hughes flew up to the yard-arm until the toggle came against the pulley. Here he was suspended for a few seconds, and then the rope was let go within board, and allowed to run while he fell from a height of about forty feet into the water. The end of the rope on board was again pulled upon again our poor Welshman appeared at the yard-arm, and was allowed to hang there many seconds "to dry" – again he was let down. This rigorous treatment was repeated until he had been three times immersed.

While, these things were going on, the ringleaders continued their correspondence with the Government respecting the terms on which they would return to their duty. These terms, as I have said, were a compliance with their first demand, without abatement or enlargement. But before I mention the settlement of this very unpleasant business, I must refer to one more incident illustrative of the spirit in which it was carried on.

In a frigate, that part of the hold called the spirit-room is situated far aft, and is thus distant from the hatchways, which open one over the other through all the decks, from the hold upward: the spirit-room hatchway opens no further upwards than through the lower deck, so that when a cask of spirits is got up, it is first hoisted thus far, and then removed to another hatchway to be got upon deck. To avoid this double operation being repeated every day when the allowance for the men was to be drawn off, it was the custom on board the P— to return the present-use cask of spirits to the provision-hold only, instead of the spirit-room. To the hatches of this provision-hold there had been a bar and padlock: over them the ladder for the accommodation of officers, passing between the lower and main-decks was placed. This ladder was of course removed when the provision-hold was opened. The key of the padlock had been lost, and the use of it and of the bar had been discontinued. As these hatches formed the foundation for the ladder, which was a thoroughfare for the officers, the hold was thought perfectly safe without this security, which, in fact, had been forgotten. Now what may we suppose the first act of the crew would be when the visit from the ringleaders of the mutinous fleet had joined our ship to them, and had superceded the authority of her officers? To break open the spirit-room? At least, to get the present-use cask of spirits on deck and drink away? It was-to get the blacksmith's forge upon deck; to fit a new bar and padlock to these neglected hatches; and to secure them and give the key to the first lieutenant.

There was another point in the incongruous state of things which I have described: the keys of the store-room and provision-hold remained with the officers when their arms were taken from them; and these keys were taken from and returned to their appointed place by a master's-mate, who continued to supervise the issue of provisions, and particularly of spirits, nor was the bung ever taken out of the cask until he was on the spot.

While the incidents which have been related were in progress, the leaders of the mutiny continued in correspondence with the Government; and as their petition was not again *"thrown under the table,"* or allowed to stand over, every thing was brought to a satisfactory conclusion in a week.

I think it was on Monday the 15th of May, which was ushered in by a fine morning, that our crew showed more alacrity in cleaning the decks, a practice which had begun to fall into neglect. The officers were more frequently referred to, and the yards were squared and ropes hauled taught under the direction of the first lieutenant; but these symptoms of a return to order did not yet supersede the un-sightly yard-ropes of the ominous red flag. It was known that Lord Howe, who was at this time First Lord of the Admiralty[1], had arrived at Portsmouth with power to declare to the men the King's pardon; and that the prayer of the petition was passed into a law.

At an early hour Joyce, and some of the other leaders with him, had gone on shore in form to wait upon his Lordship; and I believe they were sumptuously entertained at the Government-house along with the barge's crew who were to row him on board.

Soon after breakfast all hands were upon deck and in the rigging, and all eyes strained and glasses pointed towards the sally-port, from whence he was expected to embark. About eleven o'clock his Lordship's barge, carrying his flag (the Union Jack) in the bow, was seen to put off. In this boat, besides Lord Howe, there was Lord Bridport, who was the Commander-in-chief of this fleet.

This barge, attended by other boats containing the delegates, left the shore and rowed out with that appearance of majestic slowness which is given by the long-drawn stroke and the pause between with feathered oars, but which, in reality, if well executed by fourteen or sixteen strapping fellows, makes her slide through the water with great rapidity. Accordingly, she soon passed under our stern, and arrived on board the

---

[1] *In a subsequent issue of the United Service Journal, the following letter was published: Mr Editor, - In your last Journal is the continuation of "Recollections of a Sea Life, by a Midshipman of the last century," which are highly entertaining and instructive, but he is in error in asserting, page 136, that "it was known that Lord Howe, who was at the time First Lord of the Admiralty, had arrive at Portsmouth," &c. &c. Earl Spencer was First Lord of the Admiralty at the time of the mutiny in 1797, having been appointed to that situation in the room of the Earl of Chatham, who had succeeded Earl Howe in July 1788. Earl Howe was sent by the Admiralty as the negociator, if such term may be allowed, between the Government and the refractory seamen, and, as is well known, fully accomplished that desirable object. [signed] Q in the Corner. February 6th, 1832.*

Royal George, the flagship of Lord Bridport. The two noble Admirals retired to the cabin.

When Lord Howe was prepared to read the King's pardon, which was subsequently read by the Captains of each ship to their respective crews, the ship's company of the Royal George were summoned on the quarter-deck. They were not long in obeying the summons, but anxiously crowded to hear the contents of this interesting document. The afterpart of the quarter-deck was occupied by the officers, and an open space left in front of the cabin door for the First Lord of the Admiralty and the Commander-in-chief. When all was ready, they came out of the cabin together, and Lord Howe took from his pocket the paper and began to read. Lord Bridport whispered something in his ear. He immediately stopped, and returned the paper to his pocket. He then addressed the leaders of the mutiny, and pointing to the yard-ropes, which still hung from the fore-yard-arms, told them that he could not declare the King's pardon to them while that signal of mutiny remained aboard.

The yard-ropes were forthwith ordered to be taken down, and this movement was accompanied by a signal which made it simultaneous throughout the whole fleet. The King's pardon was then read, and the officers resumed their authority and their duties. Before Lord Howe quitted the ship, the men requested that they might be permitted to give him three cheers at parting; but this was objected to, on the ground that cheering had been so lately used to express unanimity in a mutinous combination. Hoisting the Royal Standard, and saluting it with a royal salute of twenty-one guns, was substituted as a more appropriate expression of a return to loyalty and obedience.

Thus happily ended, in its main source, the mutinous spirit which had been diffused through the fleet; but the ramifications of it were yet destined to give some trouble. The impulse which had issued from the Channel Fleet as a centre, was felt in a greater or less degree by our fleets or squadrons at most of the foreign stations. In some it was suppressed with a high hand, and it was put to rest in others when an account of the amicable settlement at Spithead reached them.

At this time Sir John Jervis, afterwards Lord St. Vincent, commanded a fleet off Cadiz, and having timely intimation of what was going on in England, had established throughout his fleet a system of such rigid discipline and surveillance, that it is not easy to imagine how intelligence could be communicated or plans concerted between men in ships, separated as they were by being constantly at sea, and the little necessary intercourse among them by boats being so strictly watched as it was. They did manage to hold intercourse, however, and had arranged plans for rising in mutiny. This intention was frustrated by the premature display of it on board one of them. The attempt at mutiny was suppressed on board of her, and those who appeared to be most prominent in it were secured; they were immediately brought to a court-martial, which pronounced sentence of death on them late on Saturday.

On the following morning (Sunday), the ships suspected of being the most mutinous, formed a squadron to windward. That having the condemned men on board was one of them. The signal for their execution was flying at the top-gallant-mast-head. The forenoon of this day displayed the novel and impressive sight of these unfortunate men hanging in the squadron to windward; the in-shore squadron, under the command of Rear-Admiral, afterwards Lord, Nelson, engaged with the enemy; and the main body of the fleet occupied in the customary Church service, which was indicated by each ship carrying the signal[1] for being so employed.

These prompt measures put an end at once to the intended mutiny, and an early opportunity was anxiously watched for and taken by the men in each ship, to destroy and throw overboard the agreement of the crew to rise in mutiny. This agreement was written in the centre of a sheet of paper, and the names signed around it in the manner of a *round robin*. Thus, by the decision, promptitude, and energy, of Lord St. Vincent, was prevented a mutiny, which might have ended in the loss of that portion of the British fleet. Such a termination as that at Spithead, was not to be expected a second time.

---

[1] When the crews of ships in a fleet are summoned to prayers, the ship or ships carry a signal, to prevent being unnecessarily disburbed.

Fortunately for the country, the Government was prepared to oppose with decided measures the mutiny of the North Sea Fleet, which followed, declaring the mutineers rebels, and putting an end to all terms with them, excepting those of unqualified submission.

It was enabled to do this the more freely, by having the mutinous ships at the Nore inclosed within the numerous shoals that form the intricate channels by which the river Thames is approached. Whether the turbulent men who were the instigators of this second mutiny ever could have persuaded the seamen to go with them into an enemy's port, cannot be known; but by the time that the desperation of their own circumstances might have induced them to act thus, they had lost much of their influence with a large portion of the men. It was, however, put out of their power to make the trial by that wise expedient of the Government, which caused all the buovs that marked the channels to be removed, notwithstanding it put a stop to the commerce with the port of London; but this, indeed, was an evil which the mutineers themselves had the power of causing.

In this state of things, a voluntary offer was made by the ships of the Channel Fleet, (so lately mutinous themselves,) to be led against those which should continue to hold out in their rebellion at the Nore. This unanimous offer showed that a combination still existed among them, which might have been dangerous, if the leaders had continued mischievously disposed, but as it was, this graceful act of loyalty may be termed the last act of their mutinous association. The great body of the men in most of the ships at the Nore, would have returned to their allegiance sooner than they did, but it was, of course, the interest of those who had become obnoxious by taking the lead, to prevent them from doing so; and such as were disposed to rebel against that usurped power which ruled them with an iron hand, were for a time afraid to speak their minds. This position of things could not last.

"Those —s are a b—dy sight worse to us than our officers," was an expression which escaped one, and was responded to by many. The Repulse and Leopard were the first two ships which acted upon this feeling; cut their cables, and ran into harbour. Others followed their example, until the denounced rebels formed but a small number. When the Repulse started, she was fired at by the mutinous ships, and her first lieutenant, Mr. afterwards Captain, Delans, who had assumed the command, had his leg shot off. This officer was very much beloved by the men; and it is stated that when the rebellious ships commenced firing upon the Repulse, a new mutiny, of an amiable nature, arose in her, the object of which was to force Mr. Delans below out of the way of the shot, and the men were in the act of forcibly putting him down the hatchway, when his leg was taken off.

I soon afterwards happened to join one of the ships which held out to the last, and was, perhaps, the most obstinately rebellious amongst them. This ship was commanded by a good easy man, but the benevolence of feeling that made him averse to order any punishment, was accompanied by a want of sufficient energy to preserve his ship in that state of discipline which would prevent inferior officers from ill-using the men, according to the practice of that day. Sometimes, indeed, he would get into a passion at the abuse of this practice; but then he was goaded on by complaints from the officers, and was glad to relieve himself from the necessity of punishing the men by permitting them to do it. When the mutineers took possession of this ship, they pointed the forecastle guns aft; and one of the women on board, I am sorry to say she was a Scotchwoman, (Scotch Maggie,) put the poker in the gally fire, and when hot, handed it up as a match that would not miss fire. The men were more moderate, however, for seeing that they were joined by the marines, and that the officers formed too small a number to oppose them, they went aft on the quarter-deck, where the good old captain was with the officers. As the men came aft, he got into a violent rage, defied them, accused them of ingratitude, and called for a ballast-basket, filled with pistols, which happened to be in the cabin, to be brought out. Under the circumstances described, the men did not wait for them to be loaded. They closed upon the captain and officers, and, partly by persuasion partly by force, they made him retire into the cabin. One fellow, while he held him by the arm as he was hustled into the cabin, putted him gently upon the shoulder in the manner that one would move a child out of danger.

I fear, from what has been said concerning the state of discipline in this ship, that our captain's charge of ingratitude against these men could not be established. There was amongst them one to whom the charge did apply. This man, some little time before, had belonged to another ship, and in her had been tried by a court-martial, of which his present commander had been president, on a charge that would have affected his life. Every body was satisfied as to the truth of the charge, but his benevolent judge, having a fastidious care in a case of life and death, found some objection to the evidence. By this means the man was acquitted, and he happened afterwards to be drafted into this ship. His captain, seeing this fellow amongst the foremost of the mutineers, took out his pencil in its silver-case, and reminding him that that pencil had saved his life, gave it to him. When the fellow went below, he sold it for a quart of grog.

Soon after the mutiny at Spithead was ended, we sailed in His Majesty's ship P—, for a cruise off Havre de Grace. This partook of the tiresome nature of a blockade. The vicinity of the French coast enabled the vessels which we chased to get off into some creek or inlet under the numerous batteries with which the shore is lined. We only succeeded in making one capture, and she was towed out by the boats from under the fire of these batteries. The sanguinary Government of France had been unable to enforce the law which they attempted to make, that no prisoners should be taken; and it remained for the iron sway of Buonaparte to add perpetual and hopeless exile to the fate of prisoners of war. This sullen and savage practice had not yet been introduced to break down the chivalrous amenities with which modern warfare had been graced. But neither the horrible reign of the slave Robespierre, nor even the more powerful despotism of Buonaparte, the grand object of whose life was the destruction of England, had power to supersede altogether those feelings of generous rivalry which had subsisted between the people of the two great nations which were so long opposed to each other.

The capture of our prize gave occasion to send a flag of truce on shore with her crew; and there remained in this part of France, at least, some of the generous spirit of Henri Quatre. The boat returned to us containing a large basket of strawberries as a present. This little incident corresponded with the generous disposition to avoid inflicting individual suffering which was still shown by England in forbearing to interrupt the French fishing-vessels. These vessels, and the thousands of industrious persons whom this occupation supported, were permitted the unfettered exercise of their trade, and they passed and re-passed our men-of-war with the same freedom as they did each other.

One morning on the clearing up of a fog, and while we lay perfectly becalmed, we found ourselves so closely surrounded by multitudes of these vessels, that our Captain thought it a prudent precaution to beat to quarters, and to order the men to wear their arms until a breeze should spring up. In the mean time, a boat was lowered down and sent to examine those which were nearest to us, and to search for arms. Our precaution was in this instance unnecessary; but the temptation to intercept our merchant-ships in going up Channel, arising from the facility of turning these fishing-boats into privateers, or giving to privateers the same appearance, was too great to be resisted. This practice was followed. England could no longer permit such a cloak for the destruction of her commerce. The fishing-vessels were involved in all the penalties of war. They were swept from the coasts of France and Holland; or the few that remained were shut uselessly up in their creeks, and thousands of unoffending and industrious men were reduced with their families from affluence, honestly earned from the treasures of the deep, to penury and want.

CHAPTER VII

HAVING finished our cruise off the French coast, I was removed from the ship in which I now served, to one of the North Sea fleet. This desired event was brought about by my friends, who, as soon as they heard of my shipwreck, made application for my being received by the good old gentleman who commanded His Majesty's ship B—. A place had been kept for me in her, but there were not many mid-shipmen in the P, and I did not obtain my discharge until I had seen some summer and winter cruising in her. I had lost most of my clothes when my former ship was wrecked, and my funds for supplying this deficiency were somewhat limited. Added to this, I felt that I had been thrown by this accident among strangers, so that I had to learn what is called to stand upon one's own feet. I dare say I was all the better for being made to know that we cannot always walk upon smooth pavement, but I was nevertheless very happy in the prospect of removing to His Majesty's ship B—[1], under the kind and friendly old officer who commanded her.

When I joined this ship at Chatham, she was full of shot-holes, and bore all the marks of having taken an active part in the great battle which had just been fought; and every day I was reminded of the ill-luck that had prevented my coming in time to be in this engagement, by hearing it fought over and over again.

It was late in the spring of 1798 before His Majesty's ship B— again took her station off the Texel, to watch the motions of the remaining Dutch fleet, which were by this time refitted and ready for sea again; but not ready, it would appear, for another action with the British fleet. Here I passed a very agreeable summer. I had then nothing to do with the anxieties of a blockade; my cares were limited to the details within the ship. In these I was taught to believe that I could now be of some use, and was more employed than older hands who had not been roughing it in small ships; in short, I began to fancy myself a man, and to perceive that I was not treated like a youngster. I was, consequently, very proud and very happy.

---

[1] *HMS Belliqueux, Captain John Inglis.*

The monotony of our blockading duties was much relieved by our frequent communications with England; to say nothing of the transports which at least twice in every month brought us loads of bullocks and vegetables, and the never-failing supply both of amusement and additional provender furnished by our fishing-nets.

Capt. Hall mentions in his "Fragments" the mistakes which the world on shore are under about the sea-life of sailors necessarily supplying them with plenty of fish; and this certainly is a great mistake, speaking generally, but not so as it respects the North Sea Gropers, as the fleet stationed there were called. I have known us catch in one night, enough to allot a pound and a half to every man in the ship, which was altogether about 800 pounds of fish – turbot, brill, soles, skate, and Dutch-plaice – all the bottom-loving, groping varieties; but it was rarely that the more nimble cod or haddocks were entrapped in our traul.

In fine weather our usual routine was, after manoeuvring the fleet, and sailing in various order and points of bearing along the coast, from Camperdown to the Helder Point, to stand in shore to the southward of this point, to a situation from whence the enemy's ships could be seen over the low neck of land which this point terminated. After seeing them all snug, the fleet wore off, and after standing out a little, the Admiral made the signal of permission given to fish; and shortening sail, and backing his main-top-sail, got his traul out, in which his motions were followed. Our success in fishing was various, depending chiefly upon the ground we were on, but something, too, on the management of the ships, to keep them going at a proper rate; and sometimes when the traul was put out during the watch of an awkward officer, and had been dragging along the ground for two or three hours, and a glorious haul was anticipated, it would be found to have been all the time on its back by coming up in that position, and, of course, empty.

For the sake of such as have not been employed on this fishing service, I may mention that this disaster is likely to happen in two ways. First, if the traul be lowered when the ship in lying-to has come up to the wind and has got stern way. And, again, when she has headway, if the rope be veered out by jerks and starts, so as to pull violently on the traul and to be slack alternately. If we suppose the fleet lying-to, main-top-sails to the mast in open order; and your traul in its place, ready for being lowered by its hawser, led through a block on the main-yard, with its travelling guy led in through the port abaft the gangway; the time for lowering it is, when the ship, having fallen off, shows that she has gathered headway by beginning to come to again. If the helm has been a-lee, it should now be put a-mid-ships, and the fore-top-mast stay-sail hoisted, if not already set: veer away the traul-rope freely, but steadily; pull to the guy, and keep the ship going with as equal a rate as possible, consistently with preserving your station. The best rate of going for the traul is about one knot and three quarters. If the wind be light, the fore-sail, main-top-mast stay-sail, &c. may be set to keep up this rate, as the main-top-sail must remain aback.

I have mentioned that this ship was one of the worst of the mutinous ships at the Nore. Her state of discipline had not been improved since the battle of Camperdown, in which the men, having wiped off the stain of their former misconduct, fancied themselves privileged to commence a new score of credit upon the indulgence of their commander. Some changes in the officers after this battle were also unfavourable to the discipline of the ship. A disposition to licentiousness and riot was shown on the occasion of her being paid before she left the Nore to resume her station off the Texel.

This disposition to licence and disorder was rather more glaring than usual; but everybody remembers that pay-day was a day on which all the drunkenness and disorder which could not be prevented, was wisely not seen, if kept within any moderate bounds. The *perpetual imprisonment* that was necessary to insure the *unlimited* compulsory service of seamen, could not by any contrivance be enforced when it became necessary to dock a ship. The unavoidable intercourse with the shore would then have made the attempt futile. Accordingly, when a ship was in want of repairs, it was an object that the men should have as much pay as possible in arrears before she should come into harbour; and no payment was made until the ship, being ready for sea, had gone out to a roadstead, and was prepared to start again upon service. Then the men were paid, according to their own phraseology, with the top-sail sheets in one hand, and the money in the other. In the case of their having been on foreign service, they sometimes received five or six years' pay in this manner. If the service to which the ship was destined did not require instant dispatch, it was not usual, however, to sail till the morning after pay-day; so that, during this interval, Jack had an opportunity of relieving himself from the intolerable evil of going to sea with all this money in his pocket.

The approaching saturnalia of pay-day are indicated soon after daylight by the approach of boats from the shore coming in thick succession towards the happy ship, until they form a fleet, which are kept off, lying on their oars, and cover some acres of water around her. Meantime the customary occupations of the morning go on; the decks are washed, and the yards squared. At seven bells, the bumboat-[1]women, who have been in the habit of supplying the ship, are admitted. And if poor old Tracy, or some other favoured Christian slopseller[2], be in the way, he is, perhaps, admitted at the same time. The tribe of Israel now become importunate to get on board, seeing this indulgence, and, probably, bring their boat quietly under the main-chains to get up by stealth, but are warned of their temerity by a volley of rotten eggs about their ears from a host of young midshipmen, while one of this party directs the pipe of the fire-engine to give them a shower-bath. Those young gentlemen are in full commission to keep off intruders by means of such missiles, and grand fun it is for them.

By the way, about old Tracy. He was a venerable-looking old man, who had proposed to the Admiralty a plan for raising the Royal George. This plan was so feasible and ingenious, that the Board had approved of it, and directed that he should be supplied with the means of executing it from the dock-yard. The attempt failed, and old Tracy distributed through the fleet a pamphlet, in which he attributed the failure to jealousy and want of cooperation in the dock-yard authorities; and managed to make himself popular as a slopseller. He used to appear

---

[1] Bumboat, a floating huckster's shop.
[2] Slops, ready-made sailors' clothes.

among the rest of the loaded boats on the morning of pay-day, seated on the top of his baskets and bales, his hat off, and his gray locks streaming in the wind, havjng a large board on his breast, suspended from his neck in the manner of a label, with the word "Tracy" on it" in letters that might be read at the distance of a cable's length. Eight o'clock arrives. Permission is given for the slopsellers to come on board, and now begins the general scramble. They are only admitted at the gangways, and bales, boxes, and baskets are tumbled up there with wonderful dispatch. Meantime attempts are made to board at other unauthorised parts; so the youngsters, who have by this time renewed their supply of rotten eggs from their friends the bumboat-women, are in full operation; and when the decks are sufficiently crowded with these interlopers, their further inroad is necessarily opposed by means more effectual than the rotten-eggs and the fire-engine. I do not mean that their persons are assailed by more formidable weapons, but their property, which Moses values beyond all personal consideration, is in jeopardy. The boxes and cases which he is endeavouring to smuggle on board, are pitched unceremoniously down the side, to take their chance of falling in the boat or in the water. Happy are they who have bv this time got all their store on board; and thrice happy those who have been able to secure a stand for its display upon the quarter-deck under the eye of the officers, where it is safe from any attack of open robbery.

To do Jack justice I must repeat here, that during the war there were in most ships, mixed with the true-bred sailors, a portion of convicts and of men who could not be kept in order by being flogged at the cart's tail, and were, therefore, sent to us by the civic authorities; this, I trust, we shall not see again. But independent of these conscience-seared fellows, we must admit, that a sailor would not regard the robbing of a Jew in the same light as robbing any one else. Between the sailors and the Jews there exists what is called a natural antipathy: – natural enough when the causes are investigated. Of this indefatigable tribe, who are always on the alert to offer *accomodation* to those who have money in prospect, a large portion made the anticipated pay and prize-money of sailors the object of their rapacity; and as Jack thought that signing his name, or making his mark, was an easy mode of getting the means of having a cruise on shore, he often chewed the cud of bitter disappointment on discovering that all he had obtained for his twenty or thirty pounds of hardly-earned prize-money, was a slop jacket and trowsers, a watch worth a pound sterling. and a few slippery shillings with *promises* of more. The regulations respecting the payment of the navy threw obstacles in the way of Moses and his operations in that branch of his business; and, indeed, our tar was placed more out of the reach of his machinations in a man-of-war than any where else.

While the sailor persevered in the hopeless endeavour of eluding the press-gangs, for the purpose of sailing in merchant-ships, during the interval between his voyages, he was wholly in the hands of those miscreants. A ship returns from the West Indies, for instance; such of her crew as are fit for the navy, if they have escaped the search of men-of-war in the Channel, are landed on some retired part of the coast: they have retained some of the pav which they received in the West Indies; a gold piece, perhaps, in order "to have their friend in their pocket when they return to England." Let us suppose one of them landed on the coast of Essex: he proceeds warily, like an animal conscious of being hunted, he avoids the sea coast and large towns, and is grievously disappointed to find that "the friend in his pocket," being a foreigner and unknown, is of no use. He calls at one farm-house and tells his tale, and his hunger and thirst are relieved. When he is forced to make a similar appeal to another, he is informed that "there is a *poomp* in the yard." As he approaches the neighbourhood of Wapping, still greater caution must be exerted to avoid the press-gangs; but in doing this he is resolved not to trust to the Jews, who have taken him in before. Without any definite notion, however, of a safe course between this Scylla and Charybdis, he goes on until he feels the urgent necessity of getting change for his gold piece. For this purpose he may have recourse to a Jew, without trusting him further; accordingly he is tempted by the inviting advertisement of "highest prices given for gold and silver," to enter a door over which hangs the quaint device of three suspended balls, which means that the chances are two to one against the articles pawned there being ever redeemed. The gold piece is exchanged for some silver coin of the realm, considerably under its value, but with an appearance of friendliness and fair dealing that induce Jack to believe that this Jew, at least, must be an honest man; so, with this impression of his integrity, he, with all the simplicity of undisguised confidence, answers the artful interrogations of Moses, tells him be received the pocket-piece in the West Indies, from whence he has just arrived; and that twenty pounds were still due to him by the merchants for his voyage; that, considering himself so rich, he felt the more distressingly the hardships he had endured since he landed on English ground. Our sailor is knowing enough, however, to conceal from his interrogator that he has the note for this sum sewed up in his jacket. He means to take an opportunity of presenting this note himself, by which means he will get pos- session of the money in his *own* hands, and if he be wanted for another voyage he will have the influence of the merchants to protect him from the press. That is, he will be turned over to their own Jew crimps, who will fleece him less than a stranger, because they are in some degree responsible to the merchants, being in their pay; and being thus paid, they can afford to manage with a smaller number of hundreds per cent. in their dealings with the men. But the road between him and the merchant's counting-house is beset with dangers, and he is glad in the mean time to accept the kind offer of the friendly Jew to conduct him to the house of a civil landlady, where he will be safe from the press-gangs. Jack lives in clover there for a couple of days, during which his friend Moses waits upon him assiduously, providing all he can want or wish. He soon finds his wants to exceed the amount of his ready money; thus he feels the necessity of cashing his note, but the Jew informs him that the press-gangs are constantly in the way, so that he is glad to entrust his friend with his order on the merchants for his wages. When this note has been duly endorsed by Jack, and accepted by the merchant, Moses is in no hurry to get it cashed, but can let our sailor have any accommodation in the mean time; and recommends, first, that he should have a suit of long clothes to enable him to sally forth securely. Jack see no end to twenty pounds! But when he has, in fact, received the honest value of *five*, he finds the balance brought against him, and he

is again in debt. The land-lady informs him there is no trust —
and Moses tells him that he must provide him a ship.

"A West Indiaman ?"

"No; a nishe Easht lndyman."

"An East lndiaman ! I would as lief go in a man-of-war."

"Vell ! yon can take your choish."

" Can't you get us a West lndiaman ?"

"No; I only get Vest Indymen for them as can pay for them;
and, beshidesh, you are in my debt, which must be paid out of
the two months advansh." And poor Jack is obliged to submit
to that which he would consider the greater evil of the two,
were it not that he sees a possible termination to it at the end
of the voyage.

I have endeavoured here to draw a picture of the relation
in which the Jews and sailors stood to each other. The Jew,
although an evil, made himself a necessary evil to the sailor,
an incubus that hung over him in all his motions to watch for
his unguarded moments; and many were they, to keep the word
of promise to his ear, and break it to his heart. No wonder,
then, that in an ill-regulated man-of-war the property of the
Jew, when brought there for sale, should have been liable to
attack from the sailor in a manner more direct than the
recondite methods in which his own had been assailed by the
Jew. Happy then, as I said before, was he who got a stand for
his slops, watches, and buckles upon the quarter-deck.

It happened that in His Majesty's ship B—[1], on her pay-
day at the Nore, one of those Jews who was the last to get his
goods on board, was puzzled to find a place for their display,
until some of the sailors put the gratings on the main
hatchway, and thus formed a vacant area, of which Moses
greedily took possession for his shop. He was little aware of the
insecure foundation on which he stood; for the sailors had
taken care not to place the gratings in their grooves, but to lay
them down in such a caper-cornered manner, that a gentle pull
upon a rope that was secretly attached to them, would trip up
the whole. Accordingly, when the riches of this son of Israel
were spread abroad, the rope was pulled upon, and down they

---

[1] *HMS Belliqueux, commanded by John Inglis.*

went to the regions below. Moses, by some mischance, miraculously escaped his intended fate, and was left on the brink of the precipice with uplifted hands, and features the picture of despair, bewailing his vanished riches. The combination to rob the Jews seemed on this occasion to have been extensive; and some articles were plundered even from those who were on the quarter-deck. An investigation into these robberies took place; and though many were implicated by strong presumptive evidence, our Captain considered the proof to be made out clearly against one man only; a fine-looking fellow, a thorough-bred sailor, who had but a few months before recommended himself to the notice of his Captain and officers, by his spirit and activity in the battle of Camperdown. This consideration induced the Captain to regard his offence rather as a frolic than as a crime, and he was punished with *one* dozen lashes. In consequence of this lenity, the First Lieutenant, who had joined the ship since the action, reported, in a letter which be afterwards wrote to the Admiral, complaining of the discipline of the ship, that robberies were committed with impunity on the quarter-deck before the face of the officers. Besides the general complaint of want of discipline, the object of this letter was to request a Court Martial upon a young scoundrel who had often been turned over to the Lieutenant's hands for punishment. This boy, in conjunction with one or two others of the same stamp, by way of being revenged, cut the gun-tackles and breechings on the main-deck, one night off the Texel, when we were tumbling about to a strong gale of wind ; and the guns were only prevented from finding their way through the opposite side of the ship, by the vigilance of the gunner's mate, who discovered the mischief before they had quite gone adrift. Our benevolent and conscientious Captain thought the evidence deficient against these follows; and they were allowed to remain unpunished, until this letter of the First Lieutenant brought one of them to a Court Martial.

The Court, after hearing the Captain's statement, delayed sitting until it had been submitted to the Admiralty; but the Admiralty ordered the trial to proceed. Our Captain considered this step as an encouragement held out to those under him to supersede his authority, was very indignant, and resigned his command soon afterwards. Not-withstanding the irritating circumstances which thus attended his quitting public life, he retired to the bosom of his family at a good old age, with the laurels of Camperdown fresh on his brow, and in his domestic circle found a better field for exercising the benevolent virtues of his nature, than a man-of-war afforded; for how consistent soever such virtues may have been with the duties of managing his ship, and laying her alongside of an enemy, they were but ill-adapted to the task of keeping in order the turbulent and incongruous elements on board of her. Thus, however, I lost my second patron in the same manner as mv first.

Soon after these events, considerable changes were brought about by a new Captain and First Lieutenant, and now also commenced a prospect of some real service in the expedition to Holland. This turned out to be one of the ill-fated efforts of the Government of that day, to force our friendship upon our neighbours who were *oppressed* by the French, the expense of which forms a part of that millstone of eight hundred millions which hangs upon us and paralyses all our efforts.

As usual, we failed to convince our friends, the Hollanders, that they were oppressed; or, at least, if they were, they chose to remain so; for although, when we entered the town of the Helder, all was gratulation, joy, and orange ribbons, there was no person there to receive us and express that joy, but women, who had been left to take care of the property; and there was not a man to be seen capable of bearing arms. The progress of this expedition, so far as it depended on the army, was, as usual, marked by that devoted gallantry which insured success at its commencement; and the success continued as long as the enemy bore any reasonable proportion to their number. But it seems to have required no great foresight to perceive, that as our small army marched onward, from their resources through the swamps of Holland, their numbers lessening by every success, and still more rapidly by sickness, and as the enemy fell back upon their resources and upon the armies that poured out of France to their succour, a time must come when no devotion or gallantry could avail.

On the 27th of August[1], the troops under Gen. Abercrombie approached the shore, full of zeal and alacrity. The army of the French and Dutch was drawn up behind a low range of sand hills that formed the upper extremity of the sea-beach. The boats, therefore, as they approached, and the sea-beach on which the men landed, were exposed to a destructive fire from an unseen foe. As the men jumped from the boats, they formed into little parties like magic. These little parties rapidly augmented in bulk, and gallantly charged upon the lurking enemy; who, driven from their position, suffered in their retreat for the mischief they had done, and our army remained masters of the coast and of the Helder Point, with its town and batteries. I think it was here I first heard the old joke about a guardsman roughing it upon a beef-steak and a bottle of port. An old general-officer in the boat was very facetious on this score with a young guardsman. This was the first campaign of the latter, and since that day the guardsmen have been well practised in roughing it upon less dainty fare than a beef-steak. The general officer was not among the 500 that were killed upon the beach; I never learned whether this first essay of his young friend was not also his last.

On the 10th of September, our troops were again attacked by an increased force of the enemy, and again beat them back. Soon after this, the Duke of York landed to assume the supreme command, and brought also a reinforcement to the army, including 20,000 Russians. The first battle fought under his command was on the 19th of Sept. The Russians were, as yet, our faithful allies and pupils. A Russian army was thus associated with ours. The strong force of the enemy to be attacked on the 19th, was in front of the right of the allied army. The Russians had this post of honour assigned to them, whilst Gen. Abercrombie, with 15,000 British troops, was drawn off to the left. The reason of this arrangement, I know not. The Russians, however, behaved well to begin, and drove the French from their position; or, perhaps, the French, knowing their men, and looking to the result which followed, politely withdrew. The Russians piled their arms and began the work of plunder. The French re-attacked them under these

---

[1] 1799.

circumstances; and would have destroyed the whole of them, had they not been saved by the prompt assistance of a few British battalions who had been in reserve. The Russians regained their arms, and the French were again repulsed. The field of battle remained to the allies, but no further progress was made till the 2nd of October. The Duke resolved to advance upon the enemy along the line of the sea-beach. He was deterred from this movement on the 1st, by a strong wind rolling the surge of the sea up the beach, so as to make it impassable. On the 2nd, this obstacle did not present itself; and Sir Ralph Abercrombie, with the British, was now placed in the post of honour, and led the advance. The enemy were attacked and driven from all their posts to a line ten miles from that which they had occupied, and left to our troops the towns of Alkmaer and Egmont-op-Zee.

On Sunday the 6th of October, it does not appear to have been the intention of either the French or English Generals that their armies should be engaged. The French were, probably, disposed to wait for additions to their army, which were now pouring in from the south. They were, however, already strongly reinforced. The main bodies of the armies were at some distance from each other. The generals and some of the field-officers had gone to church at Alkmaer, to return thanks for their success. An impatient disposition, or, perhaps, some mistake, induced the videttes of the opposite armies to fire upon one another. The pickets came up to support the videttes. Party after party was sent forward to support the pickets, until about three o'clock, a general and sanguinary engagement was the consequence. By this time, the officers had joined their respective brigades; but it is said, that this was not done without some hurry and scrambling. Night put an end to this battle, which was not attended with any decisive result. Each army occupied its former position.

This was the last battle to which the Duke of York deemed it proper to expose the army under his command; thinned and attenuated as it was by sickness more then by the loss which these battles had occasioned, though that was also considerable, while the number of the enemy was augmented hourly by fresh troops. Soon after this action, the information which was brought to the Duke of York respecting the magnitude of the enemy's approaching succours, caused him to resolve upon falling back.

Chapter VIII

While the army under the Duke of York was retrograding, the fleet, under the command of Sir Andrew Mitchell, was prevented by contrary winds from entering upon the intricate navigation of the Zuyder Zee for some days after landing the army. On the approach of the expedition, the Dutch fleet had retired to the uppermost navigable part of this sea, and moored themselves in a line-of-battle along the edge of a sand-bank. They consisted of eight sail of two-deckers and some frigates. After two or three days of anxious expectation, the wind at last came to the north-west, which, with the assistance of a flood-tide, enabled us to round the Helder Point close under its numerous guns; which, being now in the hands of our friends, were no longer formidable to us.

The British fleet consisted of nine sail-of-the-line. But it was the policy of England at this time to nurse the growing power of Russia, who was then (and was always expected to be) her faithful ally. Consistently with these views, a Russian fleet had been for some time cruising off the Texel in company with ours, and exercising with them in all their evolutions. To prevent the accidents which might have happened from their awkwardness, they were not admitted into the British line; but formed one by themselves to windward, where they followed our motions. Two exceptions were made: the Ratvasen, commanded by a son of the first Scoto-Russian Admiral Greig, and the Mistizloff. These two ships had become so expert, that they were admitted into the British line, and formed a part of it. They were, therefore, added to the nine ships which were destined to sail up the Zuyder Zee. By the way, these northern allies of ours sometimes amused us with odd feats illustrative of their power of stomach. For instance, when their ships were being repaired at our dock-yards, the caulkers could never keep any *slush* in their troughs. This said *slush* was a compound of the dregs of train oil, cleaning of lamps, and such like palatable stuff. The caulkers carry it to dip their caulking chisels in, to prevent the old pitch from sticking to the iron, while they drive the oakum into the seams with them. Now, the contents of these slush-troughs were too tempting a morçeau for the

Russians. Accordingly, they were always emptied, if not watched with due care by the caulkers. The taste of the officers was, sometimes, more refined. A handsome dinner was got up for a party of them on board the B—. One, who sat near the head of the table, was asked if he would take some fish; but having settled that point with himself upon observing a butter-boat filled with oyster-sauce, and large enough to have served a small family as a soup tureen, he said he should like that. It was accordingly handed to him, and he forthwith gobbled up the contents, to the great dismay of all the fish-eaters.

The fleet of nine sail of British and two sail of Russian two-deckers having rounded the Helder Point, our course now made the wind fair for us. It increased to a strong gale. But in this inland sea the water was smooth, so we dashed merrily along, although there were not many inches between our keel and the bottom. The British ship America, and one of the Russian ships, getting a little out of the deepest part of the channel, stuck fast upon the ground. This reduced the English ships to the same numerical force as the Dutch fleet, with one Russian ship in addition. Soon after this, the masts of the enemy became visible, with their large Dutch revolutionary ensigns flying. These, like the French, were tri-coloured, and bore a cap of liberty in the upper corner. But the blue, white, and red, were ranged horizontally instead of vertically.

Agreeably to the quixotic zeal with which Britain exerted herself to save her friends from the oppression of the French, our declared object. in this expedition was to restore to the good people of Holland their legitimate Prince. But I have mentioned, that our army, at least, had found no great disposition in the good people to receive him. However, in following up this intention, the Prince of Orange's flag was hoisted in our ships alongside of the English ensigns; one side of which, being thus darkened, it seemed encumbered with its accompaniment, and to want the daring freedom with which it was wont to wave alone.

About noon we had reached within four miles of the Dutch line, and would have been alongside of them in about half an hour. It blew fresh, and it was therefore deemed proper to have a second reef in the topsails, that they might be handy for setting, in case the cables should be shot away after we had anchored alongside of our *friends*; so at this time the fleet took in the second reef of their top-sails by signal, and furled the top-gallant sails. This was soon done, and we again resumed a steady course. Already the men began to trim and blow their matches, to take off their jackets, one to tie a handkerchief round his head, another to tie one round his waist; and all began to tuck up their sleeves, and to arrange and rearrange the tackle of their guns; while a chosen portion stood by the stoppers, and attended to the cable, which was led out of the stern in order to anchor in the manner of St. Paul (by the stern). The brief space which now appeared to lie between some of us and eternity seemed too long, and all appeared eager to span it over. At this time a boat was seen to be rowing towards us from the Dutch Admiral's ship. She, as well as the boat, displayed a white flag. Almost simultaneously with the display of this flag, the signal "Prepare to anchor," flew from our Admiral's mast-head. In two minutes the preparative was hauled down. The fleet rounded to, shortened sail, and anchored together, retaining their relative positions to each other. These movements acted on the men like the touch of a conjuror's wand. Before – all were full of life and alacrity. After the anchor was let go – the men heard the orders that were given, and obeyed, but without the buoyant spring and the vigorous action which a few minutes before had been so conspicuous. There was one old rough-visaged sailor at my guns who had neither seemed so much excited by our approach to the enemy, nor so much cast down by our halt as the rest. When the ship was anchored, and we had returned to our guns and were standing there idly, waiting for permission to leave them, this old son of Neptune broke out into kind of soliloquy, the tone and manner of which showed that he fully partook of the general disappointment.

" I knowed that the —s would not fight."

" Knowed it?" said another, who understood him literally, " How did you know it ?"

" How – why, because they had enough of it two years ago. And, besides, I didn't like that 'ere b—y Orange flag hung up alongside of ours. I knowed that no good would come on it!"

Our sailor in these opinions had exactly hit upon the causes of the disappointment. The Dutch sailors had, by this time, discovered that the tri-coloured flag, with the cap of liberty in the corner, brought them no more liberty than an Orange flag. And, besides, as our sailor observed, they had had "enough of it two years before." So that they would not fight against the Orange flag. In this dilemma, the Dutch Admiral displayed his flag of truce, and despatched a boat to beg twenty-four hours to consult with the authorities at Amsterdam as to what should be done in consequence of our carrying the Orange flag. The answer of Sir Andrew Mitchell we understood to be, that he might have one hour to consult the captains of his fleet; at the end of which, if he did not surrender to the British flag, or hoist the Orange one, we should be alongside of him. Before the hour elapsed, an answer came to say, that he surrendered to the English flag, but had no Orange flag to hoist.

An officer from each of the British ships was forthwith sent with a boats crew to take charge of the one which had been appointed as her opponent in the enemy's line. Here an anomaly took place which I have never been able to unriddle. These officers took charge of the Dutch ships with the revolutionary colours flying, and they remained up until sunset; at which time they were hauled down, as were the British ensigns, in the usual manner. I never learned why the Dutch colours were allowed to be kept up so long. Perhaps it was conceded to their Admiral for his civility in surrendering with so little trouble, in order to be less offensive to the good people of Amsterdam, whose spires were in sight. Next morning, however, the Orange flag was hoisted by the British authority on board those ships.

The America was still hard and fast upon the ground; the boats of the fleet were despatched to her assistance; the B—'s launch was sent with a stream anchor; the anchor was dropped in the proper direction, and the end of the cable taken on board of her. By it she hove off and joined the fleet. I have great pleasure now in the recollection that I was employed in this boat; but it was a rainy and blustering morning. We had left our ship about six, and did not get back to her till one o'clock. I "felt all the vulture in my jaws," and I fear I had then more satisfaction in sitting down to a dinner, which was also my breakfast, than at having been an humble accessary in saving his Majesty's ship America from peril. It was a day or two after this, before the wind admitted of our returning to the Helder. When it did, we sailed down the Zuyder Zee in company with our prizes, thus easily won.

Aa the crews of the Dutch ships would not fight against the flag we carried, it would not have been fair to have made prisoners of war of them. On our arrival at the Helder, therefore, they were landed, that they might fight against the French; but whether they did this, or went home to other occupations, or joined the French army, I never heard. These were only the common men; the officers landed on their parole; and the petty officers, not being sufficiently honourable to be trusted on parole, but too honourable to declare for the Prince of Orange, were taken over to England and shut up in prison. I am afraid that their consistency was never rewarded by the French Government, who were the real rulers of Holland at this time. We remained at the Helder for some little time, which was occupied in putting the Dutch ships into sea-worthy trim for their passage across the North Sea. The first retrograde movement of our army was the signal for taking these ships out of the way of becoming a bone of contention. According to what I have said, then, about the motions of the army, it must have been about the 6th of October that I happened to be in a boat employed to bring off some rope from the Dutch arsenal at the Helder, when an aide-de-camp, who had come from the army in great haste, was there enquiring for a boat to take him off to the Admiral. Many officers asked him questions about the situation of the army, as we had heard the firing of a general engagement. The aide-de-camp was, of course, not communicative; but his silence clearly showed that our army was no longer advancing, and the hurry to get off the Dutch fleet (into one of the ships of which I was now sent) showed that our surmises as to the import of the aide-de-camp's communication were correct. By this time a number of British men-of-war had arrived at the Helder, and each of those which had brought the Dutch ships down the Zuyder Zee was appointed to take charge of her protegee across the North Sea;

so his Majesty's ship B— came off with the Dutch ship Batavia. We called her then His Serene Highness's ship, and were all very loyal and wore Orange cockades. But as these vessels never returned to Holland, and as those among them that were thought available, were fitted out as men-of-war for our service; and, moreover, as I got fourteen pounds for my share in this expedition three years afterwards; I presume that our Government, upon second thoughts, determined that as the Prince of Orange had no country, he did not require a fleet of men-of-war.

However, off we came with His Serene Highness's ship Batavia. After passing the Helder Point, we kept along the shore for some distance towards Camperdown, in order to round the shoals which lie southward from the Texel Island. As we sailed along the coast, we could perceive symptoms of some of the comforts of a seat of war. We saw, over the low range of sandy hills, volumes of smoke arising from a town on fire. Peiton was, I think, the name which our pilot gave to this town.

In the zest which the "glorious news" of the Gazette Extraordinary gave to the old port over which it was discussed, these little items in the matter of warfare served but as landmarks. "How happy is Britain to escape being the seat of war!" is a sentiment which has been expressed; but, I believe, the happiness has never been duly appreciated. To have one's house plundered by his friends in one day, and burnt by his enemies on the next, for the crime of supplying their opponents, must be no joke. British armies alone always paid for the supplies which they took, as our national debt must remind us; and yet, after all this, we are told by officers of the army, who must have had opportunities of knowing, that the French, who levied contributions without paying for them, and who had no reserve in their atrocities, if the demanded supplies were not forth-coming, but who bowed to, and danced, &c. with the wives and daughters of the citizens, were better received than the upright, but inaccessible Briton. There must have been a good deal of the spaniel in these our allies; for all people, amongst whom our armies went to meet the French, were assumed to be such.

We brought our prizes safely over to England, and I rejoined my ship. When I first joined this ship, I fancied myself to have become a man – I was now sure of it, for I had been appointed to take charge of a watch in conducting a Dutch line-of-battle ship across the North Sea. I was further confirmed in this good opinion of myself by being rated a master's mate in a vacancy which happened in the B— at this time. Had I got this promotion under the good old gentleman on whose account I had joined her, I might have thought it a matter of favour; but I was more proud of it as it was. Before the ship was sent upon any other service, it was again necessary she should be docked. To explain this, I must mention, that in beating out from the Nore after her former refit, the Pilot managed to run her upon a sand- bank called the Ooze, where she lay till the next tide. Notwithstanding the name of this shoal implying softness, it was hard enough to knock off the false keel of our good ship, and to occasion her constantly to make water enough to find wholesome exercise for her crew, in the way that the cough of Sir Sampson Maclaughlan did for him, according to his wife's opinion in her answer to the benevolent condolence of Aunt Grizzy – "It does him good, child; it is the only exercise he gets."

Having above conducted the reader so near to a sea-fight, and then disappointed him, (which, by the way, was the Dutchman's fault, and not ours,) I think I must here give him an account of one which did take place some years afterwards with our *friends* the Russians, who had then become our foes; and of which I had an opportunity of knowing the details. In the summer of 1808, when Buonaparte, not contented to rule Spain through her corrupt government, insulted her people by an attempt to supersede the name of that government, and thus made his first false step, he had previously despatched a Spanish army of 10,000 men, under the Marquis de la Romama, to second his views in the North, or more truly to send them out of Spain. The presence of this army on the shores of the Baltic, and other threatening appearances to our allies the Swedes, whose fleet was thought very inferior to that of Russia, then at war with them, caused our Government to send a considerable fleet into the Baltic, under the command of Vice-Admiral Sir James Saumarez, now Lord de Saumarez, for their protection. While the main body of this fleet remained upon the coast of Sweden to guard it, and to obtain information of the

102

disposal of the enemy's force, a detachment of it under Rear-Admiral, now Sir Richard Keats, was stationed in the *Belt* (that part of this inland sea which lies between the islands of Zealand and Funen). This officer succeeded in opening a communication with the Marquis de la Romana, and ultimately embarked his whole army, who were thus relieved from their banishment, and returned to join their brethren in Spain. Two ships had also been detached under the orders of Rear-Admiral Sir Samuel Hood, to join the Swedish fleet, and co-operate with them. These two ships were the Centaur (his flag-ship) and the Implacable, commanded by Captain, now Sir Byam Martin.

Having proceeded to Carlscrona, the principal naval arsenal and harbour of Sweden, Sir Samuel Hood learned there that the Swedish fleet had put to sea; but there was no account of the Russians having yet done so. However, while the Centaur and Implacable were completing their water at this place, accounts came that the Russian fleet was at sea, and that the Swedish fleet had put into a port on the coast of Finland. A strong breeze blew directly into the harbour of Carlscrona, out of which no line-of-battle ship had ever beaten before, the entrance to it being long and very narrow; and the Swedes had taken it for granted that it was impossible. *"On ne peul pas."* But imaginary impossibilities did not deter Sir Samuel Hood. The two ships did beat out. I am afraid to say how many tacks it required, but I think the number was thirty-nine.

The southern coast of Finland, which forms the northern shore of the gulf of that name, is much indented by bays and creeks; and near to the lower extremity of this coast, where it rounds off into the Gulf of Bothnia, the creeks are formed by numerous islands. Into one of these creeks the Swedish fleet had put, when they heard of the Russians being at sea; although it is not easy to understand what the Swedes had gone into the Gulf of Finland for, if it was not to meet the Russians. But this mode of warfare was very prevalent then among those nations, as it had been in former times with Britain also, when modes of attack were discussed at great length, and some advantage always expected to be gained, before a battle should commence; instead of going direct to their point in the straightforward bull-dog fashion of later years. A little before this time, I saw an amusing instance of the sort of warfare to which I have referred, between the Danish and the Swedish flotilla of gun-boats. His Majesty's ship A—, in which I then was, lay at Malmo, for the purpose of escorting the convoys of British merchant vessels, which passed into the Baltic through the channel between this corner of Sweden and Copenhagen, which is opposite to Malmo. The channel is called the Malmo passage. The part of this passage navigable for large ships is narrow, and the whole distance across, from Malmo to Copenhagen, is such, that each can be seen from the other, though both lie low. The Danes and Swedes have each their flotilla of gun-boats at those places respectively. It is quite clear, that two hostile ports so situated, could not both long continue to have such flotillas, were it not for the care with which they nurse them, and the indulgence of each to the other by retiring when it appears to be incumbent upon his opponent to attack.

His Majesty's ship A— had escorted a large convoy through the Malmo passage into the Baltic, and was returning to her anchorage at Malmo. She was in the narrowest part of the channel, when it fell a dead calm. The Danish gun-boats sallied forth to attack her, and forming themselves into two divisions, took positions upon each quarter from which they might have almost destroyed her with very little risk to themselves, if they had advanced about 500 yards nearer than they did. They would thus have chosen a distance at which their long thirty-two pounders would have banged through the ship with every shot; and the sharp and low points which they presented to be fired at could not easily have been hit by our guns at that distance; but they kept at the extreme range of their guns, and did but little damage. A light air of wind enabled the A— to get out of her helpless situation in these narrows, and to gain her anchorage at Malmo.

By the time she arrived there, the Swedish flotilla were getting under way, and stood out very boldly to attack the Danes, who were now retiring towards Copenhagen. The Swedes followed them with great demonstrations of zeal, and cheered us as they passed. The chase of the Danes continued until they had nearly reached their own side of the channel. It now seemed proper etiquette that the tables should be turned, and that the chase should now proceed the other way. Accordingly, the Danes having put about, and stood out to meet their pursuers, we expected to see some hard fighting, but this was not intended; the Swedes put round also, and stood back to Malmo, with the Danes chasing them, till they got near the Swedish shore, when it became their turn again to be pursuers; and this glorious game of humbug was continued across and across the channel for the rest of the afternoon. The Danish *Government*, however, were more in earnest, and censured the commander of their flotilla for not going nearer to the British ship. We understood that he was superseded, and one of more determination put in his place. The effects of this change were made apparent upon his Majesty's ship A— the next time that she was returning through the Malmo passage, when she was again caught in a calm. She was attacked in good style by this flotilla, lost all her topmasts, her lower-masts, rigging and hull were much cut up, and she had sixty men killed and wounded.

Formidable things in the smooth water of inland seas these gun- boats are. But this is not the account of the battle which I promised. When his Majesty's ships Centaur and Implacable had succeeded in beating out of the harbour of Carlscrona, the wind was fair for them, and they were not long in reaching the port where the Swedish fleet lay blockaded by the Russians. The position the blockaders had taken up off the port admitted of those ships passing them. They did this, and sailing into the port, joined the Swedes. The Swedish and Russian fleets had nearly the same numerical force as to ships of-the-line. I forget the exact number, but I think it was twelve or thirteen of each. The Russians, however, had more frigates, and some of them were heavy ships with guns on their gangways. Besides this difference, two of the Russian ships, the Angel Gabriel, and another tremendous-looking three-decker, having guns on their gangways, showed four complete tiers of guns.

No sooner did Sir Samuel Hood get into the port where the Swedes were, than he began his attack upon their Admiral. Not upon his ship, but upon himself *in propria persona*, to urge his going out with the British ships to attack the Russians. A great many obstacles were to be encountered. Some of his ships were in want of this or that necessary repair. All these were undertaken and completed by the assistance of the British ships. But to crown all, the water-casks were on shore, and he could not go to sea without water. The boats of the Centaur and Implacable had them on board for him that night. While these things were going on, the Russians did not like the look of two British ensigns flying amongst the Swedes. Still they expected it to be a *ruse de guerre*. But to assure themselves on this point, they made a pretence to send a frigate in with a flag of truce, whose Captain satisfied himself that the ships were really what they seemed to be. After he had joined his fleet, the Russians saw a corroboration of his account by the British and Swedish ships getting under way, and standing out on the morning of the 25th of August. It was now the Russians' turn to run. The western extremity of the coast of Revel, which forms the southern shore of the Gulf of Finland, terminates in an island. The island is set into an indentation of the land, and thus forms and protects a creek which we called Port Baltic, and the island we called Rodgerwick; but as I do not observe this island and port marked in our common atlases, I presume they are of no great note, though the island and coast are fortified to protect this harbour. From the anchorage where the Swedes had been blockaded, across the mouth of the gulf to this port, is about sixty or seventy miles. This distance, therefore, the Russians had to run before they could reach a place of safety. The wind was blowing down the gulf, (from the eastward) so that they could make a course for this port, but could not have fetched much above it. For this purpose they were nearly close-hauled on the larboard tack. When the two British ships and the Swedish fleet made sail in chase, they were a good distance to leeward as well as astern of the Russians. Before the night set in, a very sensible change had taken place in the relative positions of the British and Swedish ships. The Centaur and Implacable had left the Swedes nearly as far as they were now distant from the Russians, on whom they were gaining fast. This troubled the Swedish Admiral. A Lieutenant of the Centaur was on board of him to interpret signals. The Admiral was very desirous to know from him whether Sir Samuel Hood would engage at night. He took great pains to explain that he was very ready to fight in the day-time, but did not understand fighting at night. He was assured, however, that Sir Samuel Hood would bring the Russians to action whenever he could come up with them. The fears of the Swedish Admiral were so far groundless, that the British ships did not come up with them during the short night which followed; but when the sun rose, they appeared to him to be among the Russians. Still he wondered that no firing had commenced. They were in fact not near enough to do any good in that way as yet. The Centaur and Implacable both sailed well. In this general chase there was no restraint as to keeping stations between those two ships. There was, therefore, a fair trial of their sailing. The Implacable had the best of it. In the course of the chase she had gained about a mile and a half to windward of the Centaur, and by seven o'clock, she was in the wake of the Sewolad[1], the leewardmost and sternmost of the Russian line. She was a large eighty-gun ship. Before this time the Sewolad had tacked to get into the wake of her own fleet, and had stood on the starboard tack about half an hour for this purpose. The Implacable followed by tacking after her, and when the Sewolad again tacked to follow the Russian fleet on the larboard tack, the Implacable had gained so much, that the Sewolad passed her to windward near enough to exchange broadsides; the Implacable having stood on until she was in the wake of the Sewolad, again tacked after her.

The Swedish fleet were by this time hull-down to leeward. The Implacable, now sufficiently far to windward, was able to keep her sails *clean full*, and soon shot up under the lee-quarter of the Sewolad, where a thundering exchange of broadsides commenced. The Russian Admiral could not stand this, but made a signal, which was answered by three large ships. They bore up to succour the Sewolad. When Sir Samuel Hood in the Centaur saw this, he forthwith made a signal of recall to the Implacable, who therefore left her friend the Sewolad, and bearing up, came down to the Centaur. The two ships formed in close order to wait the result and support each other. The Russian Admiral made another signal, which recalled his

---

[1] *Modern transcription is Vsevolod.*

ships, and they all continued to stand on towards Port Baltic, while the British ships kept close astern to watch for an opportunity of attacking any stragglers.

The land on the Revel side of the gulf, at the end of which Port Baltic is situated, now hove in sight, and the Russian fleet looked up for their port; but the Sewolad, which had been the leewardmost before she was attacked by the Implacable, at which time she lost a hundred and thirty men, and had her sails and rigging much cut, never got her sails to stand well afterwards ; so that, of course, she fell to leeward of the rest still more, and when they barely fetched in to Port Baltic, she was unable to weather the point of the island that formed it, and dropped her anchor close to the coast of this island. The British ships followed the Russian fleet until they had all stood in to this port, and then bore up and ran down upon the Sewolad. She appeared to be aground, but a nearer approach showed that she had boats towing her. She had weighed her anchor, and was endeavouring to make her way round the point against the wind, which was now very light. When Sir Samuel Hood perceived the boats towing, and thereby saw that she was afloat, he observed, that if there was water for her, there would be water for the Centaur, which now steered right for her, followed by the Implacable.

As the course of the British ships lay down the coast, and the head of the Sewolad was directed up, the Centaur approached her nearly end on. The wind, being light, made the approach slow, and it was quiet. There was no useless firing of guns to lull the light wind into a calm, but all that could be courted into the sails was made use of. The boats which had been sent to tow the Sewolad dispersed. The foremost carronade on the forecastle was the first gun that was fired. The signal for its discharge was the crackling noise made by the flying gib-boom of the Sewolad, as it broke its way through the fore-topsail of the Centaur. Her helm was now put hard a-starboard, and as she grazed her way across the hawse of the Sewolad, carried away her flying gib-boom and gib-boom in succession, until her bowsprit hung in the main rigging of the Centaur, whose triple-shotted broadside went off gun by gun as they came to bear upon the bows of the devoted Sewolad, until you might have driven a coach and six through them. Had this continued when the hulls of the two ships came in contact, the burning powder blazing up between them, would inevitably have set both on fire. Sir Samuel Hood, therefore, gave orders to board the Sewolad, whose bowsprit now lay over the poop of the Centaur. The Russians made a pretty good stand for a little time upon their forecastle, but were soon overpowered, and submitted, although not until four of the Centaur's men had been killed, and about twenty-eight, including the first lieutenant, wounded. During this encounter both ships had fallen aground.

Capt. Martin, perceiving that no good could be done by a third ship coming in contact with two vessels thus entangled with each other, and with the ground, anchored the Implacable in a most seamanlike manner a short cable's length to seaward from them; and running a stream cable to the Centaur, hove her off as soon as she had done her work. The boats of both ships were now employed to take the prisoners out of the *wreck* for the purpose of burning her. When they had commenced doing this, it was perceived that the Russian fleet which had anchored, were again moving, three of them being already under way and standing out. Sir Samuel Hood then despatched a boat with a flag of truce, to say that it was his object now to save the lives of the remaining crew of the Sewolad, and particularly of the wounded, but if the Russian fleet moved, they must instantly be sacrificed by her being set on fire. The three Russian ships again anchored. The removal of the wounded and of all the prisoners was completed, and the Sewolad, being set on fire, made her final exit in great splendour.

CHAPTER IX

IN the last Number of these Recollections, I have been led
into a digression which made a leap over nine or ten years. I
now return with pleasure to the happy. days of the cock-pit.
Capt. Hall's admirable "Fragments of Voyages," has drawn the
veil from the common observation, which had been too long
received upon authority, that "our school-boy years are the
happiest of our lives." If I were to fix upon the happiest of mine,
I should say the three last years of my time as a midshipman;
and were I to select from that period the happiest days, I think
they would be found in this winter, while our ship was in dock
at Chatham. Our residence during this time was on board a
hulk, whose "ruined walls" inclosed accommodation that was
sadly deficient in that desideratum of an Englishman called
comfort; but which, illuminated by a "purser's dip," that only
made darkness visible, were lighted up by the gay and buoyant
spirits within; so that, if the dismal appearance of our home
was referred to, it was in some joke that served to enliven the
scene, or to contrast it with the nice order of our own berth on
board the B——. Yet there were marks which showed that
midshipmen of taste and industry had been here before us.
Where the cobwebs and patches of whitewash were broken
away, there appeared glimpses of ornamental painting, that
spoke of other times. But notwithstanding the brilliancy with
which memory can burnish up the walls of the floating cells
which could then supply us with a happy home, it will not be
supposed that we were slow to quit it for the allurements of the
shore. These were abundant, even at Chatham; but our
vicinity to London put that world of fascination within our
reach. I happened to have some friends there, as most people
have who have any friends at all; and several times I managed
to prolong a twenty-four hours' leave of absence to three or four
days. The shorter term was all that the first Lieutenant, or
even the Captain, had the power to grant, although the ship
was in dock; but in such a case a tacit understanding was
frequently given, that *they* would not call the delinquent to an
account who might break this strict rule of those busy times,
provided that he first obtained this negative sort of consent.

"I wish to go to London for a few days, Sir?" "*I* cannot give you leave. Take care that the Admiralty do not call you to account." The chance of the Admiralty knowing the motions of a midshipman were readily encountered.

In the short interviews which these trips admitted of my having with young females of the civilized world, I fell into a fancy, under which I remained during the whole time of my active employment at sea. This was, that such young females were, actually and *bona fide,* angels. The brief mortality in this world of the fairest of God's creation, which at the age of eighteen we recognize in words only, has now been long too familiar to my conviction; but as regards all the other attributes, I have still the happiness of remaining under the delusion, if indeed it be one. In being led by the fascination of this alluring theory, I presume that I was under the same circumstances as many others of my brother officers, who in such short intervals, and even for some time after the war was ended, had too sublime an idea of the perfections of such beings, to feel themselves at home in their company, unless it happened to be with some young lady of a frank disposition, the intimate of a sister, perhaps; and then he was sure to fall in love; and sometimes to commit the egregious sin against the object of his attachment, of getting married to her; to say nothing of the sin he thus committed against Lord St. Vincent and His Majesty's service, by depriving the King of a good officer, and dividing that devotion which he owed to the navy alone, where in those stirring times he ought to have remained "all as one as a piece of the ship." I was fortunate enough never to think of incurring this climax of evil to a young naval officer; but of course I tumbled most profoundly into love on such occasions.

In one family of young ladies, whose frank and friendly manners had superseded that sublime veneration to which I have referred, there was one for whom it still remained. Some degree of relationship justified the intimacy, and the elder sisters freely kissed me at parting considering me to be a boy, although I had ceased to think myself such. The youngest did not take advantage of this privilege of kindred. This sent me back to the ship with a heavy heart. I was not such a goose, however, as not to see that this omission might have arisen rather from diffidence than dislike; so I made up for it by banishing my own absurd share of the diffidence at a second leave- taking. But the good sense, or good feeling, or diffidence, or altogether, which prevented anything like a declaration of love, in this case, as in many others, preserved for me the friendship of the lady to the end of her life, which was terminated, but too soon, at the distance of thirty years afterwards.

I returned to my ship this time with a lighter heart, but still pensive enough, until the bustling duties of fitting out again came upon us. Our ship was now got out of dock. My station as a master's- mate called upon me for more exertion. The stir of these active occupations soon loosened the hold of the boyish dreams with which my fancy had been entangled, and prepared them to be washed off in the first salt-water cruise we should encounter. Having touched upon this ticklish ground, it is now high time to be off to sea again. So up anchor, and let us proceed on our voyage.

There was no longer a Dutch fleet to blockade in the North sea. Our ship (a 64) was rather small for the line-of-battle that watched the French fleets. What was to be our next destination, was a question that interested us all. Orders to proceed to Spithead gave a prospect of something new; and orders, when there, to take under charge an outward-bound convoy of Indiamen, opened to the young and ardent imaginations on board, the expanse of the wide world, and the anticipation of many a brilliant scene, which, if then seen and enjoyed in the wildness of untutored hope, still preserve a fascinating, though a calmer charm in the mirror of recollection. It was in the beginning of May before our convoy were all assembled, and we then dropped down to St. Helen's with them to wait for a wind. Before we did this, our ship's company were paid their arrears of wages, and this pay-day went off with less disorder than the former. This time our friends, the Jews, were undisturbed in the exercise of their vocation, and by means of certain liquid elements, contained in small bladders enveloped in neat paper bags, and sold under the denomination of pounds of sugar, they had the power of inviting Jack to become their customer, and at the same time blinding him to the mystification of their accounts in a manner which made up for the losses sustained by their brethren at the Nore.

I ought to add, for the honour of Jack, that the bumboat-women, landladies, and all others who had trusted him, were duly remunerated before the remainder of his money went in this way. Many of these creditors had come round from Chatham for this purpose. I believe there was but one exception to their being all honestly and liberally paid. There was one fellow who made an objection to his account, in rather a Joe Miller sort of style. I am not sure whether Joe was before him, but he certainly stuck to his point with the gravity of an original. This was a Dutchman who had entered for our service. Having built rather largely upon his anticipated pay, he had made his visits to the bumboat-woman rather often – so that, besides the score for loaves of bread, red-herrings, sausages, and "*pounds of sugar,*" there appeared upon his account a considerable number of dittos. Now, he acknowledged to all the above-named articles, and paid for them fairly, but he declared most forcibly that he had never had any ditto, nor could he be brought to understand what the word meant by all the logic of the bumboat-woman, or those who advocated her cause.

Having assembled our convoy at St. Helen's, we rode out here a heavy gale of wind from the westward, after which, a wind partially fair brought us to Torbay, where we anchored to wait for a better. The gale I have mentioned had sent the Channel fleet in from off Brest; and the prevalence of westerly winds had detained squadrons and fleets bound to all parts of the world. To these numerous fleets of men-of-war and merchant-ship, were now added our superb convoy of about thirty Indiamen.

The Channel Fleet, which were in the habit of putting in here during westerly gales, in order to save tear and wear while the French could not get out of Brest, were always kept in perfect readiness to sail "on the first *blush* of an easterly wind," according to the order of Lord St. Vincent, which commanded that no officer or man should sleep out of his ship. Amateurs from all parts of the kingdom used to assemble on the Berry-head to witness the departure of this fleet for the French coast, as they sailed majestically by that bold promontory, and so near to it, that the movements of those on board could be seen in making their evolutions.

It is said that sixty ships-of-the-line once sailed from Torbay together. I think that now was the time at which the congregated fleets I have mentioned contained that immense force, together with the splendid display of riches in the multitude of merchant ships. Next day the wind came fair, and those who were fortunate enough to be on the Berry-head at this time, saw the magnificent spectacle of those assembled fleets passing in review before them, as they sailed forth to proclaim the power and wealth of Britain in all parts of the world.

Passing the in-shore squadron off Ushant, who had been left to watch the French fleet in Brest, they stood out to communicate with their commander-in-chief; and we launched onward, leaving the Channel, and soon the European world, behind us. Night after night we continued to sink below the horizon stars which had been familiar to our view in their course all round the heavens, and to raise others which we had never seen; and exchanged the blustering elements that warred in the North Sea, and hourly called upon us for some harassing but healthful exertion, for the softer zephyrs, under which we rolled on, with sails, once trimmed, remaining in undisturbed serenity for the whole four hours. The midshipmen of the watch might be seen seated along by the lee-guns, sound asleep, fanned by the cool eddy wind from the mizen-stay-sail, under which they had walked shivering many a night in the North Sea – the mate of the watch sleeping as he walked the deck, until admonished of his error by breaking his shins on the gun-carriages; and the lieutenant almost following his example. We were now out of the track of all vessels but such as were going the same way as ourselves, and therefore not likely to meet; and as the blue expanse of water, over which we winged our way, though a sublime object, becomes somewhat monotonous to contemplate always, and as we are not always asleep in those lazy latitudes, notwithstanding the sleepy picture I have drawn; I say, as the glassy mirror of the deep becomes a monotonous study, we naturally turn our eyes to the objects reflected in it, and, like the Arabs of old, fix our attention upon the rising and setting stars, the moon, and planets, in their majestic march, until the orrery of the real heavens is formed in our heads, md referred to there with as much facility as the models which bear that name – while the observations made upon the periods of these sublime revolutions, for the purpose of finding the ship's place upon the track-less ocean, add to this contemplative study all the interest of a continued series of experiments. Enhanced by the charms of novelty, these occupations mark one of the periods that form the "bright spots in memory's waste." The charm of novelty has long gone, but I have never yet been able to send a hand to the mast-head to look out for a point of land whose longitude had been well ascertained, without feeling some of that excitement which, I presume, is enjoyed by amateurs of a horse-race when two horses are running neck and neck; and when the discovery of land confirms the minute accuracy of observations made upon the heavenly bodies to find its distance, I presume, the gratification of the observer may be not less than that of the winner at the race.

For the sake of young navigators, who have not yet set up in their heads the orrery of which I have spoken, I may mention a step which greatly facilitated the creation of it in my own. While we were yet in the northern hemisphere I soon got acquainted with the north star, and assuming him to be accurately in the pole, which is near enough to the truth for our purpose, I considered that all lines drawn from him, whatever direction they might have in relation to the points of our compass, north, south, east, or west, were south lines in the heavens and meridians of the sphere. The next step was to get well acquainted with three or four remarkable stars near the equator. This may be done by the assistance of a friend; but we were all young astronomers in the B—, and the old hands never became astronomers at all. I was therefore obliged to work out my acquaintance with these equatorial stars in the usual manner: by finding the time in the tables when they should come to the meridian, observing their altitudes, and comparing it with the known latitude. I took care to carry in my head the *degrees* of declination, and the hours and minutes of Right Ascension of the stars I had thus become acquainted with.

Having made this progress, whenever I saw a remarkable star whose name I wished to know, I ran a line with my eye from the pole-star through it, and another line from the pole-star through that one of my known equatorial friends which lay nearest in the way. The angle made at the pole-star by the inclination of those two meridian lines gave me the difference of Right Ascension between the two others; and as I carried that of the known equatorial star in my head, I thus obtained this condition of the place of the other without going below for any reference or calculation. Still assuming the pole-star to be accurately in the pole, with a quadrant or sextant I next measured the angular distance from him to the one whose name I wished to discover. The arc of a *meridian* thus measured, furnished me with the complement of the declination of my new friend. Having this approximation to his place, I was enabled to enter the table of stars contained in our old friend John Hamilton More[*sic*][1], and in it to find the name of the star I wanted.

The above loose method, abundantly inaccurate as a means of *fixing* the place of a star, I always found sufficiently near to *lead me to it*, assisted by the magnitude of the star. It had the advantage of being practicable at any time when I happened to be upon deck, without waiting until the star whose name I wished to find should come to the meridian. This he might not do in my watch, or, perhaps, not until some time in the daylight. I thus soon formed an acquaintance with all stars of the first and second magnitude; my acquaintance with them I took an opportunity of confirming afterwards in the usual manner, by taking their altitude when on the meridian, and noting the time of their being there. It is not alone in the case of a man walking without a head that the greatest difficulty lies in the first step. The commencement of an endeavour to acquire a knowledge of the stars, like the first view of an extensive museum, seems to present a task like that of unravelling the labyrinths of a wilderness; but as you go

---

[1] *[John Hamilton Moore. The Practical Navigator, and Seaman's New Daily Assistant. Being a complete system of navigation, improved, and rendered easy to any common capacity. [etc]. Published at least as early as 1772; there were many editions.*

forward, fixed points of reference are multiplied, which makes the rest easy to be acquired. We should have been much assisted in the above investigation of the heavens by a globe, or map of the stars, but we had no such thing on board; so, as I said, we made use of the real heavens instead of a model. If there was more difficulty in acquiring knowledge in this way, there was more ease in retaining it, according to the view held out by Mr. Bonnycastle, in the elegant and concise preface to his "Treatise on Algebra;" which preface, by the way, should be read by every youngster, whether his studies be mathematical or not. It is only six pages.

Having mentioned the name of our venerated friend John Hamilton More, I will not lose this opportunity of paying a tribute to his memory. His book contained the only good epitome of navigation at the time I speak of. The plan of it has since been superseded by practical *improvements*, and the useful tables it contained by others more accurate and recondite, particularly by Mendoza del Rio's having added to his truly scientific work the tables of common navigation; but our old friend John Hamilton More, whose picture, torn from its place opposite to the title-page, and ornamented with a cocked-hat and a pipe in his mouth, added by some aspirant in the fine arts, used to decorate the walls of the berth, must be venerated by every midshipman of the last century. But peace to his shade! He has had his day of fame. May this notice make his name immortal, which it cannot fail to do, standing in the pages of the United Service Journal.

Without always soaring in the heavens, there are objects of a deep interest in Nature wherever she presents herself. Among those which become apparent in these latitudes, is the teeming life of the ocean. This is made visible by the multitudes of flying fish frequently on the wing, pursued as they are by the larger fish: the skipping bonito; the dolphin, with his ever-varying hues of gold, purple, green, and orange; the large and muscular albicor, with his finely-pointed head, broad shoulders, and deep chest, and finely-tapering tail, made for strength and agility, springing through a flock of flying fish to a distance that gives the idea of his flying also, and carrying his victim along with him, or singling it out and bounding after it in a manner that would be delightful to those who are fond of coursing. To minds of a graver mood, it has suggested reflections on the unhappy lot of the smaller fish, which seem but to exist in a continued state of suffering, pursued by larger fish in the water, and attacked by birds when they take to the wing. I remember this reflection passing in my own mind, and it was not corrected until many years afterwards, when we lay in a harbour, the waters of which were, at that season, darkened by clouds of small fish. Through them the larger ones frequently dashed in after their prey, or sailed insolently among them; while the little ones darted off to all sides, and made a lane for their oppressors to pass. But I noticed that none of the debasing passions which follow the oppressions of mankind, and cause the unhappiness of the oppressor and the oppressed, prevailed here. The moment the danger was passed, they were again sporting and pursuing their own prey. So that my little friends were more in the situation of a soldier or a sailor, who consoles himself with the reflection that an inch of a miss is as good as a mile, and where the frequent repetition of impending danger tends not to despondency or unhappiness, but on the contrary, calls forth that excitement which we may every day observe to be sighed for by retired veterans. I believe the love of such excitement to be so consonant to our nature, that even the fox-chase would lose all its charms if the necks of those who follow could be perfectly secured by their being carried up to the hounds in palanquins.

Every one remembers the observation of Charles XII. when he first heard the sound of musket-balls in the air. I remember a similar illustration of the feeling I have referred to in a young friend of my own. He was seated beside me in the stern sheets of a boat as we rowed up to an enemy's vessel. The first shot she fired was well aimed, and went close over the boat. The singing of a cannon-shot is intelligible enough, even to those who have not heard it before, and does not require the question which Charles put when he heard the more insidious whizzing of musket-balls. "What noise is that?" "From henceforth that shall be my music." My young friend jumped on his feet, and clapping his hands exultingly, exclaimed that "an enemy's shot had gone over his head" in a manner which indicated that all his school-boy hopes had been realised. Poor fellow! he did not live to enjoy the music long.

I had written this much on the flying fish before I read the remarks of Bishop Heber on the same subject, in the account of his voyage to India. That gentleman, led by his habits of piety and benevolence, has been induced to believe that the flying fish are not pursued when they fly out of the water; and he considers their flying to be no more an indication of their being so chased than the sporting of lambs in a field is an indication of their being attacked by serpents. The cases arc not quite parallel, unless the serpents were as numerous as we can perceive the large fish to be; and unless also the lamb, swallowed in dozens, were known to be the natural food of the serpents, by being found in their stomachs.

We cannot shut our eyes to the existence of that which we mortals call evil, and the better way, perhaps, is to look at it in the face. That the flying fish do sport and play, and enjoy life, there is no doubt; and perhaps they sometimes rise out of the water in doing so. But in the course of many opportunities of observing, by years of sailing in those latitudes, I should be inclined to say that they did not generally fly to any considerable distance, unless when disturbed by the approach of a ship or of their enemies. It is true that the larger fish cannot always be seen; they are in the water, and often catch their victim as he falls; but I have seldom watched the flight of a flock of flying fish for any distance, without being able to detect a leap from some of their pursuers.

The view I have taken of the case, reduces the evil to the common lot of living nature; and if some seeming evil must exist in the parts, let us suppose, with Pope, that it is the least possible consistently with the excellence of the stupendous whole.

CHAPTER X

RAISING the bright constellations of the Southern Cross
and the Centaur, we sailed on among our flying-fish and their
enemies, until we arrived in those sluggish latitudes, where the
more lazy and gluttonous shark frequently shows himself,
basking in the glaring sun, or, enlivened by the splashing of an
equatorial shower, sails with his dorsal-fin above the surface;
and, by the frequent shifting of his course, seems to be in chase
of the large drops; as they fall. My excellent friend, Capt. Basil
Hall, has conveyed to his readers a most vivid picture of the
interest created in a ship by catching and dissecting one of
these monsters. He has not mentioned one circumstance,
however, that attended the first capture of this kind in His
Majesty's Ship B—. This is the celerity with which the prize
was cut up into four-pound pieces; those master spirits who
took the lead, having first secured a piece of the tail for their
own mess, because it was furthest from the stomach.

The catching of the first shark makes a capital incident in
a voyage; but when your station is among them, it would be
sorely at variance with the cleanliness of a man-of-war, to
admit on board all that could be caught.

I remember one fine calm forenoon lying in Batavia roads,
the burning sun vertical at noon, the thermometer about 100
in the coolest shade. The ordinary occupations of the men had
been suspended to preserve them from the dangerous effects of
exposure to the sun; and they were seated, or lying down, near
the port-holes, to be in the shade, and to catch any air of wind
that the motion of the ship might create. The reflecting surface
of the water, like a polished mirror, no where ruffled by the
slightest breeze, was studded all round as far as the eye could
reach, with the fins of sharks, which were lolling their lazy
way, as they enjoyed *the fine sunny day.* The sport which this
display of shark-fins promised, was too tempting to be
withstood by the middies, who, with a young marine officer at
their head, set to work, baited the shark-hook, and attached a
good strong rope to it; so that they did not require to use much
ceremony when the shark was hooked, however large he might
be. It was not admissible in such a case to add the rank smell

from the steam of murdered sharks to the annoyance already suffered from the beat, so that our young sportsmen, having hooked their victim, were obliged to be contented with pulling him up to the boat's david (one of the projecting beams at the stern, used for hoisting a boat up to). When the shark was there, they first cut open his belly, then with a sharp hatchet, released his jaw from the hook that held him, and thus let him into the water again. The instant he fell, he was attacked by those nearest to him. The more distant followed, and soon all the fins that could be seen, sailed towards that centre, and marked the water with numerous lines, in the manner of converging rays, while the devoted object of this movement was torn to pieces by his merciless brethren. Encouraged by their success, the youngsters repented the experiment, and found its result the same, until the water under the stern was crowded with sharks, as if they had been a shoal of some gregarious fish; but they were plunging, and striving, and tearing their distressed brother, with an avidity that rivalled the zest with which their *fellow-creatures* of the human race are prone to distress such beings of their species as possess not the power of resistance. The parallel has often occurred to me when I have seen a swarm of boys following a helpless maniac, and harassing him with more devilry, because with more ingenuity than their prototypes in the water.

The calm, hot, and rainy weather, in which the European is stewed while making his passage into the southern hemisphere, is a transition from the roasting of the clearer tropical sun, almost as agreeable as that from the frying-pan to the fire.

This weather occupies a belt of varying breadth, from four to eight degrees of latitude, depending upon the season, and also upon the vicinity of the coast of Africa, near to which it is broader than more towards the middle of the Atlantic.

It is always, however, on the north side of the equinoctial line; and geographical grammars, as they are called, misinform the world when they state, that the northeast trade wind prevails from the line to the tropic of Cancer; and the south-east trade from the line to the tropic of Capricorn. On the contrary, I have known the north-east trade wind to be lost in the thirteenth degree of north latitude; and the south-east trade to be met in the seventh degree of north latitude, prevailing at first much from the southward, but afterwards drawing more round to the east, until it had reached the S.E. by E. and E.S.E. from which points it continued to blow until we lost it, and took up the variable winds and heavy westerly gales of the Southern Ocean. The southern limit of the belt of calm weather is about the equinoctial line, when this belt is in its southern station, the sun having then a high southerly declination.

The fact of this calm weather lying between the trades being always to the north of the equator, probably arises from the conformation of the western coast of Africa, since, a little to the north of that line, this coast recedes to the direct west, about twenty degrees of longitude, and leaves an open ocean opposite to the southern latitudes, while the neighbourhood of the coast influences the winds to the north.

Having passed this troublesome belt, we met with a south-east trade, which, after sundry gentle, but unsuccessful efforts, at last settled in a moderate steady breeze. A portion of our convoy, five sail, were China ships. Our business was to escort them to China, and to see the other part of the fleet only as far as their course lay on that route, and beyond the numerous cruisers of the enemy which were nearer home. We had started late in the season for making the direct passage up the China sea, and had, therefore, the prospect of what is called the eastern passage before us, a much longer round. To provide for this, it became necessary to stop at some port for water and refreshments for the crew.

The Cape of Good Hope, on the one hand, lay nearly in our track, and Rio Janeiro, on the other, was but little out of the line which the south-east trade forces ships to make in crossing it. This trade is a drectly foul wind, but its limits must be crossed, in order to get into the latitude of the rattling westerly gales, that will hurl you along to the eastward afterwards.

The belt of latitude which this south-east wind occupies, is better crossed by not keeping your ship close to the wind: for although she thus looks up more to the southward, yet, by making less distance and more lee-way, she may make less southing: besides, the more you are to the westward, the more easterly, and, therefore, the less unfavourable will this wind be in a given latitude. There are limits to this rule, however, which will vary with circumstances. But if we suppose a ship to get this trade when she is to the westward of the twentieth degree of longitude, *and not so far west as to be in danger of falling to leeward of Cape St. Roque,* I should think it a good mode for discovering the best course to steer, to try your ship at six points, six and a half, and seven points from the wind; and, if it be from the eastward of south-east, say seven and a half or eight points.

Try her rate of sailing on these points, and set off the increasing distance with the more leewardly course, making proper allowance for the leeway; then whichever point of sailing gives the most southing, that is the point to steer upon, without regard to how much or how little westing she may make; for the westing, though a loss of ground, is soon made up for when you get out of the trade wind, and the great object ought therefore to be, to cross its limits as quick as possible.

We had nothing to do with this nice point. Permission being given to the ships bound for India to part company, we left them to make the best of it, and as Rio Janeiro lay under our lee, we steered away with our five Chinamen a point or two more to leeward, and thus gradually parted company with them. A general diffusion of joy was spread through the ship at this movement. Rio Janeiro was then a port but little frequented by British ships. Though belonging to our friends, the Portuguese, its Government partook of the jealousy with which the blind avidity of the Spaniards had endeavoured to monopolise the riches of South America.

But few of our seamen, therefore, had visited this port, and none of the officers. The few buccaneers, or their successors, (men who had been engaged in what was called the forced trade,) who happened to be on board, became of great consequence in the ship by the information they were able to give, scanty though it was. Some of the more intelligent were even consulted by the captain before he resolved to bear up for Rio Janeiro, and their accounts stimulated the interest which attends the anticipation of visiting unknown regions; but their glowing descriptions fell far short of the extraordinary beauty which distinguishes this paradise, of which neither pen nor pencil, nor even the more animated powers of relation *viva voce*, can give an idea adequate to the reality. Our anticipations were brightened by the mystery which was associated with conjecture in the mind of a European, on the eve of becoming acquainted with this unknown land. But some events were to intervene before our impatience was gratified, the most fearful of which was a narrow escape from a projected journey to the moon. We had likewise a successful encounter with an enemy's squadron.

While these prospects enlivened the inmates of the midshipman's berth, there was one unhappy exception. One poor young man had drunk too deeply of the fascination referred to in my last paper during our long retention in harbour. He had not, like others of his messmates, been contented with sipping honey from the edge of the cup; but, like the unwise bee, he had plunged overhead, and rendered himself incapable of any vigorous or manly exertion to free himself from the evil that involved him. He was most thoroughly and irrecoverably in love, and what was much worse both for himself and the object of his attachment, he had sworn eternal constancy, and formed one of those hopeless engagements to marry when his means should permit, which become more hopeless by the entanglement preventing the power of acquiring those means. He was a young man of mild and gentlemanly manners, and before this time, of a lively disposition. His dejection on leaving England was the subject of many a rally from his gayer messmates; but as we increased our distance from the spot to which all his thoughts were riveted, his despondency became more overwhelming, and drew pity from the most reckless of his companions. These circumstances were but little known to the Captain and the superior officers, until the young man got so bad that he became unable to perform the duties of his station. I say unable, for his case was actually disease in the common acceptation of that word. The surgeon pronounced it to be such under the name of bypochondriusis, which sounded very learnedly to us. Before this, our poor young friend got into many scrapes on the subject of his duties, and bore sundry *wiggings* on that score which did no good; but after his complaint got a name he became privileged, was never called upon, and spent his days, and, I believe, his nights too, in reading poetry and novels, for he could not sleep. At last he grew incapable even of these occupations, and used to wander from one part of the ship to another more like a ghost than a living being, until he fancied that he was going to die, and accordingly took to his bed, where he seemed in a fair way of realizing his expectation. Our surgeon, a very good fellow, wherever he may be now, (his name was Williams,) came down to attend him; but instead of giving him a passport to the other world, insisted upon his going up to the wardroom to dinner. This was accomplished with some difficulty; partly by persuasion and partly by force, he was carried up and seated at the wardroom table. There the change of scene and some lively conversation which the Surgeon and other officers addressed to him, for the express purpose of driving the blue devils out of him, made him so for forget his sorrows that he held up his head and took his dinner like the rest; and after drinking a glass or two of good wine, a fiddler, who was in waiting, being introduced and striking up a merry tune, our poor hypochondriac, instead of dying, jumped up and danced most heartily.

This susceptibility, however, was but another proof of his disease, and he soon relapsed into his former despair, in which state be remained until it was announced to him that he should return to England by the first opportunity.

While we went on our way to Rio Janeiro, some of the ships that left us were to touch at the Cape of Good Hope; and into one of these our poor messmate was put, to find his way home to England by that route; and I verily believe it was this joyful change in his views that prevented him from dying at this time. On our homeward-bound voyage, we heard at St. Helena, that he had been unable to get a passage from the Cape to England before his means of subsistence were exhausted, and that he had endeavoured to support himself by setting up a school; but had failed in this also. I have never heard of him since.

The gentle commencement of the south-east trade had, as yet, hardly assured us of its existence, when we were threatened with another calm; but the light airs of wind, when they came, arose from the true quarter, and we had no rain.

The horizon was tolerably clear all around – the look-out-man at the mast-head called out, "A strange sail on the larboard bow-and another on the larboard bow – and another – and another" – until we fancied that we had fallen in with some large fleet. "Young gentlemen, away up, and see what these ships are." In half a minute there was a midshipman at each mast-head. I happened to go to the fore-topmast-head, and got into the top-gallant rigging beside the man who was seated on the yard. "Well, where are they?"-" I can't see any of them now, Sir. There, there, Sir," I applied the little glass that I had brought up to my eye, and saw her vanish into thin air. "There is another, Sir." I watched her motions, and observed her to vanish in the same way. I now recollected having seen whales blow in the gulf of St. Lawrence, and it struck me that these shiplike apparitions could be nothing but the columns of spray sent up by the blowing of whales. I hailed the deck to say so. As they came nearer we ascertained them to be a shoal of these creatures of the spermaceti kind. Two little South Sea whalers had continued to accompany us along with the five Chinamen when we parted from the rest of our convoy. They ventured to ask permission to hoist out their boats; so up went their signal to that effect, and our affirmative flag granting the permission, the boats were soon despatched. We would gladly have accompanied them, but we were obliged to content ourselves with mounting the rigging and watching their motions.

If any sport of the sea may bear an analogy to fox-hunting, the catching of whales can alone be compared to that prince of all land-sports the boar-hunt, in which success must depend wholly on the energy and dexterity of the hunter, and not on his hounds.

The boats were engaged for some time in the endeavour to get near enough to their game, each armed with their harpoons attached to lines of 120 fathoms long, with the addition of a spare line in the boat. These lines, made of the choicest hemp, are carefully laid up, very limber and strong, and about the thickness of one's finger, an inch and quarter in circumference. Besides the harpoons, each boat was also armed with *lances*. These are harpoons without barbs, of which we shall presently see the use. One of the boats succeeded in

126

harpooning a whale. The attempts to bold him fast with the strong small line, would have been equally futile and fatal to those in the boat who should venture it; accordingly, he was allowed at first to have his full swing, and dashed away with forty or fifty fathoms of the line. Great care must be taken to keep this line perfectly clear for running, and a sharp hatchet is always ready in the bow to cut it on the instant should it catch anything to stop it. This precaution is necessary for the safety of the boat; for if it were neglected in such a case, the whale would soon get her under water, where, being in his own element, he would have the advantage of his assailants. When the whale has made bis first dash off, and the length of the line run out prevents bis motions from affecting the boat so suddenly as when it was short, the bowman catches a turn with the line round a timber-head which stands erect in the bow of the boat for that purpose; the steer man having first with his *oar*[1] turned the boat's stern, so that her head is directed towards the course of the whale.

The bowman now begins to check the running of the line round the timber-head, and veering it out more and more slowly, makes the boat's motion partake of that of the whale, and at last holds the rope fast. The whale has now to tow the boat with eighty or a hundred fathoms of line after him. At first he flies away with her and make her run at a great rate, and care must now be exerted by the bowman not to hold him too fast, and by the steersman to direct the boat towards him; by degrees a tow of this kind becomes tiresome even to a whale, and his speed is slackened.

I ought to have mentioned, that as soon as one boat had harpooned her whale, all the others ceased to pursue their own sport, and followed that boat with which the whale had run away; and when he had abated his speed so that they could come up with him, the lances, or barbless harpoons, came into use. Each boat rowed up to him, and watching their opportunity, threw their lances into him; being easily withdrawn, they were ready to be thrown again with fatal

---

[1] A rudder affects the course of a vessel only when she has way through the water; but it is required to alter the direction of a whale-boat when she has no way. She is therefore steered with an oar.

effect. When this stage of the process had commenced, the poor animal was soon despatched.

Some of the boats endeavoured to tow him to one of the ships, but the others, with more success, and with the assistance of a light breeze, towed the ship to him. He was hauled alongside and secured there. His head was now opened, and the *head-matter*, which is the spermaceti, (in the brain, I believe,) was soon baled out. The next operation was to strip off the blubber, which lies outside of the flesh like the fat of a hog. The men who were employed for this purpose upon the body of the whale, wore boots with long spikes in them, to keep them from slipping. They made an incision in the direction of the whale's length, from the gills downward, about eighteen inches long, and to the depth of the blubber, until thev reached the surface of the flesh or *crang*. From the ends of this incision they commenced the cutting of two other lines, parallel to each other but oblique to the direct round of the whale, in such a way, that, when continued, they formed a spiral round his body that terminated at his tail, and freeing from the crang with their knives the blubber that lay between the commencement of these spiral lines, they attached to it the tackle, which was now overhauled down to them from the main-yard of the ship. When the tackle was fastened to this end of the blubber, it was pulled up on board, while the men on the whale continued to cut the spiral lines, and to free the blubber from the crang between them, so that the end of it ascended towards the mainyard while the body of the whole revolved in the water, and the men with their spiked boots continued to march to that part of him which came uppermost, as if they had been on the outside of the treadmill-wheel, still cutting this spiral line of blubber as they went round. When the tackle came a-block, that is, when the end of the line of the blubber had nearly reached the main yard, it was cut off close to the whale, and the lower end of it being pulled on board, the whole piece was lowered into the ship and the tackle overhauled again for the next, until the poor whale was completely stripped of blubber down to his tail, after which he was left a prey to the sharks. When these busy operations were over, the master of the whaler sent us a young whale which had been taken out of the old one. It was about the size of a large cod-fish.

We fell in with the squadron of French frigates on the 4th of August, and our projected journey to the moon was interrupted three or four days before that event. It must, therefore, have been about the 1st of August of that year which completed the century. By the way, whether the year 1800 began or ended the century was a question upon which some ink was shed. After this, what is there that may not be made a subject of dispute? On the 1st of August, then, while the farmer of England was anxiously watching the progress of his ripening crops, we were ploughing our way towards Rio Janeiro, and were fairly advanced into the heart of the trade wind, with Cape Frio under our lee, and the wind about two point abaft the beam.

We had a fine day's run, the glare from a hot sun and bright sky had been tempered by a fine breeze, but we were not sorry to see them give place to the placid light of the moon and the sparkling of the stars in their dark blue vault, now variegated by the Magellan clouds and the milky way. The wind, though moderate, was enough to keep all the sails asleep, that is, it prevented their flapping idly against the mast, and but slightly ruffled the surface of the water. There was but little of undulatory motion called ground- well, of which there is always some in the open sea arising from distant causes, so that our ship appeared almost to stand still upon the ocean, though she was sliding onwards at the rate of four miles an hour, which could be perceived by the ear of an experienced mariner as he leaned over the hammock-rails to enjoy the refreshing sound of the splashing from her Lows. The officer of the short watch, from six to eight, whose charge might have been solitary enough during a snowy night in the North Sea, was not left alone. He had the captain and the first-lieutenant to keep him company: every body was on deck. Some of the officers on the poop, and some on the weather gangway, where they were at liberty to lounge free from the sacred quarter-deck. The old North Sea master with a wooden sextant, and the young astronomical midshipmen with metal ones, were busily engaged in shooting the moon. Eight o'clock came; the striking of eight bells and calling the watch warned those who had to turn out at twelve that it was time for them to retire if they meant to have any sleep. I happened to be among that number, and long before the ·harmony of the watch on deck was disturbed by sounds of alarm, I was in my hammock in a profound sleep, earned from having been up from four on the previous morning. The first watch was set, and, as I said, those who had to keep the other night watches now retired; but many of the *idlers* still remained on deck to enjoy the fine evening, or to listen to the stories of Darby Malony or Patrick Finnegan.

These were two Irishmen who had the faculty of telling quaint stories in so droll a way as to keep the whole ship's company in a roar of laughter. At first they were both accidentally placed in the starboard watch, and in a fine evening like that described, they used to take their seat on the main-deck, close by the break of the quarter-deck, and each to relieve the other by taking up the tale as his neighbour got out of breath ; but the listening watch had no respite from their fit of laughter. The larboard watch had complained with some reason of this unfair monopoly of the fun, so Darby Mlalony and Patrick Finnegan were separated, one remaining in the starboard and the other being turned over to the larboard watch; so that there was always one of them on deck. Some of the idlers, then, remained up to hear these funny stories, or to enjoy their walk on the forecastle. *Idlers* is the name given to all officers or men on board a man-of-war who keep no watch. It is sometimes an appropriate name for such officers, but it is by no means so for the men who receive it. They consist of the servants of the officers, and the cooks of both officers and men; also such artificers as are employed in their respective occupations during the whole day. In addition to the above proper duties, however, these idlers are frequently called up when any evolution is to be performed which requires the watch upon deck to be strengthened, in order to avoid disturbing the watch below. In the list of idlers the ship's barber should not be forgotten, as he is one of the heroes in the event which put an abrupt termination to the enjoyments of this fine evening. He does not deserve the name of idler any more than the rest, if we consider that he has five hundred men to shave. He had finished his day's work, and having walked the forecastle with the · sailors till he had almost fancied himself into one, and to be ready with them for any exploit of daring, about half-past nine o'clock he went below for the purpose of going to his hammock, when his courage met with a severe test.

The passage into the magazine is on the orlop-deck (that which is below the lower gun-deck). This passage is increased by strong bulk-heads, or partitions, which divide it from the store-rooms, containing rope, &c. &c. These store-rooms, and the passage leading to them, are also encased in strong bulk-heads, and the keys of the whole are kept in the first-lieutenant's cabin. Besides this, the magazine passage has three doors. There is one to be unlocked on entering from the passage of the store-rooms to the outer magazine passage; another strong door admits you to the inner passage; and, lastly, the magazine-door opens to a *scuttle*, or square hole in the deck, which allows you to descend to the magazine, so that is not easily assailed by this route. But over the inner passage, there is a scuttle in the lower gun-deck, for the purpose of conveying down the barrels of powder when they arc received on board. The scuttle on the lower gun-deck is covered by a trap hatch. This is braced by a thick iron-bar. The end of the bar has a clamp that, fitting over a staple, is secured by a padlock. It happened that the barber's hammock was situated near this scuttle, and about half-past nine he descended the fore-hatchway ladder, singing with a light heart, and bending under the hammocks, made his way towards his own, When he got before the bits, his attention was arrested by some one breathing hard close to him. He halted, and by the distant glimmer from the lantern of the master-at-arms perceived a figure bent down, and engaged in some violent exertion at the magazine scuttle. Presently the poor barber heard the clinking of an iron crow-bar, as the incendiary succeeded in drawing the staple which secured it, and felt himself confronted with the desperado, who now raised himself. Neither spoke. The poor barber was riveted to the spot, and his hair stood on end. He heard the opening of a clasped knife. A burst of imprecation from the maniac followed. This seemed to unfetter the limbs of the barber, who now bounded along the deck upon his hands and feet under the hammocks. The light from the lantern of the master-at-arms had vanished, by his going up to report that all was well below, and the barber performed a complete round of the deck in this manner, believing the knife to he so close at bis back that he could not turn aside to ascend the ladder without exposing himself to be stabbed. At last he bolted up the main hatchway, and arrived breathless on the quarter-deck; but being more occupied with the idea of the madman at his heels, than with his attempt to get at the magazine, some time was lost before he could collect himself sufficiently to stammer out something about "going to blow the ship up," and "the fore magazine scuttle." The officer and midshipman of the watch, the day-mate, who had not yet left the deck, indeed every person on deck, left the ship to take care of her-self, and darted to the fore part of the lower-deck. The hammocks on their way were soon untenanted by the alarm, and all crowded round the party from the quarter-deck, who were the first to arrive on the spot where the magazine scuttle stood open. Those who knew that about three hundred pounds of powder in cartridges for present use, was kept in the magazine passage, could now perceive that the ship was already in the power of the incendiary. With method in his madness, if such it was, he had placed one of the men's clothes-bags in such a manner as to keep a chink of the scuttle open to admit air when he pulled it to after him in his descent. He was now trying the strength. of his crow-bar at the magazine-door; but had he known of the present-use powder, where he already was, we should have been by this time on our aerial journey. Luckily he did not, and his further attempt on the magazine-door was interrupted by the scuttle being thrown open. He left his occupation, and presenting his crow-bar, declared that the first who should attempt to descend was a dead man. This was answered by the day-mate jumping down, followed by the captain of the forecastle and others, near to the scuttle, which would admit but one at a time. The dav-mate received a wound in his thigh from the crow-bar, but the villain was instantly secured and dragged upon deck. Besides his crow-bar and knife, a steel file and a gun-flint were found upon him.

Before this occurrence, he had had the character of a quiet, inoffensive man, and had never been flogged; but his messmates said that there had been a great change in his temper within a few days. He admitted his intention of blowing up the ship, and assigned us as a reason, that some of his messmates had offended him; but the follow got sulky, and would say no more.

CHAPTER XI

THE narrow escape we had had from being blown up, as recorded in my last, might have afforded sufficient material for talking until our arrival in port; but we soon met with another adventure to occupy our attention.

In the mean time the safe-keeping of the incendiary was a task that promised some trouble, and there appeared no prospect of relief from the charge until we should have completed our voyage to China, and either returned to England, or joined the fleet under Admiral Rainier in India.

On the morning of the 4th of August, as the sun rose, four sail were seen on the starboard bow. They were visible from the deck, and were evidently something more substantial than spray blown up by whales. They also kept their relative positions to each other with a degree of accuracy that excited our suspicion. Soon afterwards we could make them out to be three large ships standing to the northward. Our course lay to the south-west, so that we went on for some time crossing each · other's track, but still drawing nearer. On seeing us, they hauled to the wind on the starboard tack, by which they neared us still faster.

Our business was to take care of our convoy; and if the strangers had stood steadily on the course they were steering when we first saw them, perhaps we might not have led our convoy out of their way to look after them, and we could not have left our charge for that purpose. But their hauling up to reconnoitre us, increased our desire to know something of them. Bv eight o'clock they had seen enough of us, or at least they thought so, as they made us out *distinctly* to be a squadron of six sail of the line, and two corvettes. So they bore up, and made all sail directly from us about W.N.W. These movements looked suspicious, or, according to our boatswain, *auspicious*.

We forthwith put them down for enemies; but we underrated their force as much as they had magnified ours. Imagination, ever ready to be influenced by our wishes, as well as by our fears, and, in either case, to form false opinions, as also to confirm them when formed, made out one to be a frigate, and the two other ships to be large merchantmen under her

convoy. Their vicinity to South America, and their standing to
the northward when we first saw them, suggested that they
had come from some of the Spanish ports there,– as, indeed,
they had, – and that they were homeward bound. The two
merchant ships were therefore richly-laden Spanish galleons,
under convoy of one frigate. Had we known them to be three
whacking French frigates, I guess there might have been some
question as to the propriety of leading our convoy a dance after
them. However, up helm, and away we went in pursuit, making
the signal for a general chase. It was only altering the course a
few points to starboard, and setting the lower studding-sails.
Further signals were made for four of our five ships which
sailed best, to chase the two *merchantmen* of the enemy by two
and two respectively, while we directed our course towards the
frigate, who showed himself to be commodore by making
signals to the others.

China-men are generally but lightly laden outward bound.
Our five capacious ships were little more than in ballast-trim,
so that they went along at a good rate before the wind, and kept
pace with our old North Sea groping sixty-four; but how we
ever managed to come up with the French frigates they know
best. They had been long out, and lying in the river Plata.
Perhaps their bottoms were foul.

As the day proceeded, we visibly gained ground. We had a
steady course to steer, nearly before a trade wind, and had,
therefore, not much to do with the sails when they were once
well set. A pull of the studding-sail tacks and halliards now and
then, as the breeze stretched them, was all that was required;
so the forecastle was well attended with plenty of spy-glasses.
Even the boatswain found time to use the little one which he
kept in his pocket. All eyes were bent upon the commodore. A
movement of something was seen at his mizen-peak. The
glasses showed that the republican tricolor waved over her
stern.

'What do you think of her now, Mr. —' said one of the
officers who was near the boatswain. ' I thought she looked
auspicious, sir, and now she has hoisted French colours, and
that's some *sentiments* on it.'

A thorough-bred sailor, though one would not think it,
when we see him in his round jacket and tarry trowsers, has

nevertheless in him some latent seeds of the coxcomb ; these, when encouraged by ' *a handle being put to his name,*' and his jacket superseded by a long-tailed coat, show themselves in the use of '*dictionary words,*' with which his conversation becomes charged :-He 'can dispense *without* it.'   'That 'ere does not belong to my *apartment*,' and ' 0, you *illiterate* booby,' to a man who is passing an earring the wrong way, &c. &c.

The *'auspicious'* tricolor waved over her stern ; and seeing that we continued to gain upon her, and would certainly come up with her, she made a signal to her consorts, who had already spread some distance to the southward. Upon their answering the signal, one of them hauled up about two points, and the other with the schooner about four points, so that they now spread fast from each other and from their commodore; while each, as they supposed, was followed by two line-of-battle-ships, who also spread fast to the southward from us, while we continued steadily to pursue the commodore, followed by our fifth Chinaman, which did not sail so well as the others, and by the two South Sea-men at a still greater distance.

About four o'clock the Frenchman tried a shot at us. It fell short. In a quarter of an hour he tried another. This showed that we gained fast upon him, for it came whack through our lower studding-sail. One chase-gun, a paltry six-pounder on the forecastle, was now set to work, but had much better have been at rest, for in moderate weather, the frequent explosion, even from the discharge of one gun, has a very perceptible effect in disturbing the current of air and throwing the wind out of the sails, as it is called.

The Frenchman now opened a very respectable battery upon us, Two long eighteen-pounders out of his cabin-windows, and two long nines from his quarter-deck stem ports. And well they were fired;- slowly-one at a time; and evidently by choice marksmen. The next shot after that which struck the lower studding-sail, would have earned the prize for hitting the bull's eye, if our ship with her spread of sail had been a target for practice. It came in through the foot of the fore-top sail, passing the larboard side of the foremast, between it and the rigging. If it had struck the mass of rigging here brought together, (and it passed within a foot of it) the foremast would have been in some danger of going over the bows ; the sail upon it must have been speedily taken in to save it, and the Frenchman would have got off to assist his friends, if he had been so inclined, and our four sail of Chinamen, line-of-battle ships as they seemed, would have been in a bad way.

But a foot of a miss is as good as a mile ; and as the vital parts of a ship's rigging, or such as a single shot can do extensive damage to by hitting, do not occupy a very broad space, Mr. Clerk, in his Naval Tactics, is quite wrong in making the comparative advantage of firing at the rigging, rather than at the hull of a ship, to correspond with the proportion which the whole spread of the sails and rigging bear to the surface of the hull. Indeed, all practical men must continue to hold what he says upon this subject, and upon the advantage which ships engaging to leeward have by being enabled thereby to elevate their guns, to be utterly heterodox. Since, if ships are at such a distance as to require their guns to be elevated in the manner that this implies, to reach an enemy, they will be much better employed in keeping their men and their guns cool till they come nearer; and when ships are near enough for action, that is, when they *cannot* miss their enemy, every shot fired at the hull does mischief, while many may pass among the rigging and do little damage, In this case, when a gun is levelled at the hull, if the motion of the ship depresses it while firing, so that the shot strikes the water before it reaches the object fired at, it will rebound from the surface in the manner which the French call *ricocher*, and we (for want of a word) call duck and drake.

If the motion of the ship elevates the gun while firing, the shot will have its chance among the rigging. It is, therefore, only in the case of a ship endeavouring to get away from an enemy, or to come up with one that is flying, that guns ought to be elevated, and then never so much as to require the heeling of the ship to assist that elevation, which may be given them by taking out the bed and quoin. What Mr. Clerk says about the greater chance of hitting your enemy between wind and water, by guns thus elevated, is perfectly unintelligible. On the contrary, the ship to leeward evidently exposes her bottom to be fired at by the depressed guns of her opponent.

The other advantage of engaging to leeward, which Mr. Clerk mentions, – that of preventina your opponent from bearing up and getting away, – deserves more consideration. But if you go close enough to him to windward, and keep a sharp look-out upon him, and not look upon your fleet as a machine which must not change the relative position of its parts, – but, trusting that other ships of the fleet will do their duty like your own, close upon your opponent as he attempts to increase his distance from you, he will not find it easy to do so, unless your ship be disabled ; and, in that case, even if you were to leeward, he could easily pass you, and give you a raking broadside as he went by.

Our running fight went on for a good while, and, as we approached, every shot that the Frenchman fired came bang through some of our sails; while the only gun that we could bring to bear upon him, without altering our course, was the six-pounder. If the commander of this frigate had possessed any ordinary degree of shrewdness and of resolution, he would have retained the superiority he thus possessed until he either did such injury to our rigging as to prevent our overtaking him, or until we had got up with him. But while the advantage of presenting a battery to us so much more formidable than that which we could bring to bear on him became every minute greater as we neared him, instead of profiting by this advantage, and prolonging the time that he was most likely to do so, he rounded to and fired off a straggling broadside, most of which was discharged before the guns bore upon us.

Whiile we ran down upon him, he continued to lie to, and had time to load and give us another broadside before we]hauled up ; but the pointing of his guns now formed a sad contrast to the precision with which the stern-chasers had been fired, and it did us but little damage.

We shortened sail and rounded to at a distance which indicated that we did not wish to blow our prize out of the water. This was not right, while his colours were flying; but we were near enough to convince him that we had a double tier of guns, and this seemed to be all that he wanted to justify his striking. Accordingly, he hauled down his colours.

The two quarter-boats and the stern-boats of the B— were now lowered, and the first lieutenant despatched with them to see that they were quickly returned with a load of prisoners; and, in particular, that all the principal officers of the Frenchman should be sent by them. Another lieutenant, with a party of men to continue in charge of the prize, was also despatched by them. As we rowed up under the stem, we read the words *La Concorde.*

This name we had heard before. She had committed great depredations on our commerce. I remained on board the Frenchman, so thatnI was not present when the commodore arrived on the quarter-deck of the B—, and advanced to present his sword to our captain. The sword was politely.returned to him ; but the fine speech which this act was about to produce was interrupted by interrogations respecting his consorts. 'Ce sont La Medée et La Française, frigates de la République Française.' Our poor captain was in a sad dilemma: he had despatched his convoy in chase of two French frigates. In vain was the signal of recall hoisted. Notwithstanding the exertions made to get the French officers out of their ship as quick as possible, their desire to look after their goods and chattels and valuables made it necessary almost to use force to get them down the side; so that, when our first boat was despatched with a lot of them, including their commodore, the dusk of evening was closing in; and when it was made known to our captain that it was two French frigates of which his convoy was in chase, it was too dark, and they were too far off to see the signal of recall. Then was there a grand bustle. 'Up boats, and make sail !' So we were left on board La Concorde to make the best of it, with a serjeant and half a dozen marines, and about as many sailors, among upwards of four hundred Frenchmen. The B— hailed us, in passing, to make sail and follow her.

After a good deal of jabbering in broken English on their part and desperate French on ours, we managed to get some of the more good-humoured of our prisoners to lay hold of the braces with our men. The more grumpy fellows answered our menaces with 'Je suis Français,' or by imprecations not to be told to 'ears polite,' with a due portion of grimace to confirm their veracity. By hook or by crook, however, we got our sails trimmed, so as to make a shift to follow the B—.

It was now time to look out for what was going on below. I was dispatched, with a serjeant and another marine, to see that the magazine was secure. We descended to the lower deck, where a scene pre-sented itself that would have done credit to the lower deck of a British man-of-war, if safely moored, and enjoying the double allowance of grog that was sometimes given on the first anniversary of a victory·or during the license and jollification which prevailed on the night of the jubilee. Then was realized that sailor's paradise which he often anticipates in his favourite song:-

> " We'll spend our money merrily,
> When we come home from sea.;
> With every man
> A glass in his han',
> And a pretty girl hn His knee."

The Frenchman was certainly wanting in this last condition of happiness; but the *eau-de-vie* had made him sufficiently merry. On every chest or table stood pots of this liquor, and around them were seated groups of Frenchmen, singing as uproariously as English sailors could have done on the most joyous occasion.

A valuable fellow came in our way at this time ;–he had been a man in office under the former government, in the police department of the ship. Whether he was horrified with the violation of all those ordinances, which it had been his duty to enforce, or that he was a *rat* who wished to retain office under the new government, or whether he was really afraid of the consequences which might arise from the disorder that prevailed, I know not; but he immediately attached himself to my party. As our first object was to look out for the safety of the magazine, and as of its place, as well as all the arrangements of the ship, I was yet in the dark, my first direction to our new ally was to conduct us to it. As we approached the fore hatchway, we perceived the source from whence all the rejoicing flowed. A stream of people were ascending from the orlop deck with full pots, and another set were jumping down with empty ones. I placed my marine to cut off the ingress of the *aspirants* , and with the serjeant

140

intercepted those who had realized the happiness of filling their pots, and seized them, one by one, as they came up. Having no hands to spare, I was obliged to trust our new-made friend the Frenchman to empty the pots. I sent him on the main deck for this purpose, and handed them to him up the hatchway, as we took them from the disappointed possessors. Our way was thus soon cleared. When we got to the foot of the ladder, I discovered a little recess off the passage leading to the magazine, which admitted of a hogshead of brandy standing upright in it. A door was also fitted, which made this recess a secure place to contain this cask of spirits, to be drown off for present use: unlike the wholesome practice of the British navy, which requires that no spirits shall be drawn off but on the upper deck. Some of the crew of La Concorde having obtained possession of the key of this snug corner, had opened the door, and placed a large tub under the cask. The brandy was run off into the tub, and those who chose came freely and helped themselves. To enable them to see their way, a lighted candle was stuck, by a daub of grease, to a beam over the tub. The passage to the magazine within was strewed with cartridge-boxes and cartridges of powder.

My little party had now got possession of the premises, but were still pressed by 'disappointed suitors,' and the tub standing in the way of the door, prevented its being shut. This was a nuisance not easily removable. To upset the tub and let the brandy flow among the powder would have spread the danger; and if we had gone with it on deck, we must have left the cask, which was yet half full, to the mercy of new assailants;- so we were placed somewhat in the situation of the man that we have heard of at school, who had the task assigned him to carry over a ford a fox, a goose, and a bushel of oats, one at a time, and with safety to each. In this dilemma I made a compromise with the enemy. Two Frenchmen were very urgent to have their pots filled; I promised to allow them, if they would carry the tub to the main deck. I left my trusty serjeant in charge of the cask, and accompanied the tub upon deck; where, having performed my promise, I upset it in the lee scupper, and returned below. We found the key of the door, which we forthwith locked, and collecting the loose cartridges, put them in the magazine, and secured the doors of it also.

As I returned upon deck to report the completion of this duty, a large bone, not of a frog, but of a knuckle of beef, came whistling by my ear, and knocked a splinter out of the fore ladder, as effectually as a grape-shot would have done. I knew the direction whence it came, and noticed a gang of sans-culotte-looking fellows there, who had already made some offensive demonstrations, and one in particular, who I was pretty sure had thrown it; but under all the circumstances, I did not atop to make further inquiry.

Arriving on deck, and reporting progress to the officer in command, I was glad to perceive that the B— was not far from us, and that boats were coming from her, the wind being now so light, that they could do so without stopping the progress of the vessels.

The boats relieved us of a number of our most troublesome prisoners, of whom I took care that my sans-culotte friend of the beef-bone should be one. We also now obtained a more respectable force to keep the rest in order. Our cares on board the Frenchman were much diminished by this movement; but our poor captain, who had despatched his convoy in chase of two French frigates, it may be supposed was anxious enough. Night had closed in; they were entirely out of sight, and beyond the reach of signals.

About one o'clock in the morning we heard the report of a gun, and about five minutes afterwards saw the flash and heard the report of another in the same quarter, about S.S.W. There was no more firing. Again all was silence and anxiety for the fate of our convoy.

As the day broke, we could perceive three sail in the S.W., and soon afterwards two more sail, bearing south. They were the four ships of our convoy standing towards us-the first two having in their company La Medée, who had surrendered to them without firing a gun. La Française and the schooner had outsailed the others which chased them.

Our two Indiamen managed well to keep up the appearance of line-of-battle ships, under which delusion the Medée had surrendered. We understood that one of their officers having been a mate in a man-of-war, had still with him his naval uniform, and it was put on by those who were sent on board to remove the prisoners from the Medée. All her officers and most of her men were brought on board and secured before they were aware that they had surrendered to two merchant ships. The officers were frantic when they made the discovery. The captain of the Medée, with great seriousness, asked permission to go on board his frigate again to fight them fairly. But it is not to those who let slip opportunities of success that similar chances are again given: so the captain, if he really expected such permission, was disappointed; and his crew were safely lodged in the holds of the two Indiamen until they joined us, and we proceeded to Rio Janeiro.

The squadron which we thus broke up had been a most destructive one to our commerce. They had been out of France about sixteen months, had swept the coast of Africa, and captured twenty-six sail of British vessels. La Française got back to France, but without doing any more mischief; and I had the satisfaction of being at the taking of her some years afterwards. The schooner was an American, which they had taken, for France was then at war with the United States, and they had fitted her out to assist them in their depredations.

Chapter XII

After securing our prizes, as we proceeded on our voyage, sundry reports emanated from the French prisoners relative to boxes of gold on board La Concorde that had been broken open during the chase; and these reports were corroborated by the accidental discovery of several belts, filled with gold pieces and made to fit the body, which were found among the Frenchmen's luggage in its removal from the Concorde. A few boxes of silver were on board of her, which the officers admitted to be lawful prize. Those circumstances occasioned some suspicious-looking packages to be opened, in which more gold was found. All this seemed to confirm the idea that the statements of the men relative to boxes of gold having been broken open were true. Here, then, a question of some difficulty arose. To do anything which could have the appearance of robbing the prisoners of their private property was strictly to be avoided; but since goods, and gold for the purpose of merchandise, are made lawful prize by the practice of war, in order to injure the enemy nationally through his commerce, it could not be right to pass as individual property any large amount of precious metals found on board an enemy's man-of-war, although her officers were the merchants to whom it belonged, or pretended to be so; and much less was it allow- able when there was every reason to believe that they had become possessed of it only by breaking open the cases in which it had been embarked on account of others. Our captain, very properly, had considerable scruples on the subject, but at length resolved upon a general search. The Frenchmen were furious, at least some of them were, or pretended to be so; but one fine-looking fellow · the commanding officer of the troops of their squadron, who, being a colonel, had been admitted to a place in our captain's cabin, and who had his luggage contained there, in an immense chest,· as soon as he saw that the search was inevitably to take place, voluntarily opened this chest, and, from a heap of gold, baled it out upon the cabin table, at each time, as he laid down his double-handsfull, pronouncing 'Ce n'est pas à moi.' We were sorry for this man, because he acted so honourably; while a number of others were allowed to retain large sums only

144

because they had more hardihood in declaring it to be their own. In this search no standard was fixed upon for determining what should be considered as private property, and I fear that the vacillation hence arising in each case gave more offence than a rigid seizure would have done.

It requires the pen of Sir Walter Scott to convey a picture of scenery to the mind; but how much better are the pictures of inanimate nature conveyed by the pencil, than even by such a pen ! and how much more forcibly has that pen presented to us the scenes of human life, and placed before us, in bright and glowing colours, the motives to action in the ever-varying mind of man, where we may trace the remote incitements of our own conduct, and strengthen our good resolutions by the honest pride we take in seeing its better parts pourtrayed, and be made more alive to our weaknesses, by seeing them reflected to our view freed from the mists of selfishness, which bias our judgment in studying the original!

From the rolling swell and the fresh trade-wind of the ocean we shot into smooth water, passed the magnificent mountain which stands apparently isolated at the entrance of the inland sea, that winds its way throurh orange-groves, gardens, fountains, and stupendous mountains, clothed with the verdure of majestic trees even to the edge of the water. Sailing into this peaceful lake, the spires and the white monasteries to which they belonged appeared to ornament the leaser eminences that rise above a little recess of the land on the southern shore, and indicate the place of the town of Rio Janeiro. Off this bay we anchored, and, when the sea-breeze died away and was succeeded by the cairn of the evening, the whole scene was reflected upon the glassy surface of the water, and was more like to the reality of fairy-land than even the beautiful mirror-scene in that prettiest of all spectacles, Cherry and Fair-Star.

Our attention was soon withdrawn from the contemplation of these beauties to some of the coarser realities of life. Many vessels were anchored in the bay, and between them and us lay one large ship, wearing English colours. She attracted our attention by appearing to have a great many hands on board. A boat was soon seen to be rowing from her towards us with four oars and a personage of some magnitude seated in her stern sheets. We were upon the alert to know who he could be; and while the captain and most of the officers were upon deck on the side of the ship which he approached, the other side was covered with midshipmen, to see him and hear the news he might bring. The boat came alongside, and a tall, raw-boned figure, with prominent features, presented himself, dressed in white trowsers and blue coat with bright buttons, but which seemed to have been made for a smaller man. The first glance at his visage and appearance might have read ' Irish- man;' not 'Irish gentleman,' certainly; but one of that class who, supposing their claim to the title might be questioned, think it right to enforce it with an oath, and pronounce themselves to be ' Jontllemen, by Jasus !' Our friend arriving on the quarter-deck, looked round with a wild stare, and then, fixing his prominent eyes on the captain, and striding up to him, projected his chin into his face in a manner 1vhich indicated a disposition to bite off his nose; but, instead of doing this, he took off his hat, and said, ' I've come to report myself to your honour.'-' Well, what are you ?' 'I come from Cark, Sir.'-' Where are you bound to? ' To Batany Bay, Surr.'-' Well, well, what is your cargo?' • Khargo, Sir? I've got a *khargo* of united Irishmcn, and a very bad khargo you'll allow, Sir.'-' Well, then, you command a convict-ship?' ' I do, Sir; and I will *command them* as long as the breath's in my body. But I've come to report them to your honour: they mutinied on me, Sir.'- – Did they? then I hope you suppressed the mutiny?' ' I did, Sir. They mutinied on me, and would have taken her from me; but I went down below with my officers, and we shot three or four of them, Sir; and we quelled them. Yes, Sir, we shot three or four of them; but we did not shoot the ringleader; but we got him upon deck, Sir; –nand your honour knows that a desperate case requires a desperate *remmedee.* So I called a *council of war* of my officers, and we hanged him at the fore-yard-arm! – and I hope your honour ap- proves of it;' making a low bow.

The approbation here claimed so directly was a matter that certainly required some further consideration. However, our captain thus appealed to, as the principal British authority within reach, declined interfering in the matter, but advised the Irishman to proceed on his voyage, and lose no opportunity of reporting the circumstance to the authorities in England under which he was employed. I have no doubt that he made the proper report, but I never heard of the matter being brought before the tribunals of the country. The case would have been an awkward one if it had been referred to the conscientious, but somewhat stiff and rigid tender mercies of an English jury. Shooting three or four of them to suppress the mutiny, was all very well; but the deliberate act of hanging the prisoner was in itself a proof that the mutiny no longer existed. Yet who would say that the man was wrong? The mutineers, although quelled, would probably have been ready to break out again more warily and with better success had they not been deprived of their head in this determined manner. Our friend as quite right in his maxim, that 'a desperate case required a desperate remedy;' and he probably saved the lives of himself, the crew, and many others, by the sacrifice he thus made.

At this time the Portuguese were at war with France, if a nation can be called at war that has neither the power of aggression nor defence against her opponent but such as he receives from her allies. The two French frigates seemed in every way fit for his Majesty's service; but to have taken them to the Cape of Good Hope, our nearest colony, in order to their being fitted out as English men-of-war, would have delayed the progress of our voyage. Our allies at Rio Janeiro were desirous of purchasing our prizes, and offered a fair price for them, viz. a number of milreas, which amounted to about 18,000*l.* sterling for the Concorde, ans about 7000*l.* for La Medée. These terms were agreed upon; but when the mode of payment came to be discussed, it was found that the 26,000*l.* was to be in bills. This broke off the bargain which would otherwise have been fulfilled. I do not know how such a case might be managed now; hut in those days an enemy's vessel might be sold first and condemned afterwards, provided that her papers and the *necessary fees* were sent to the nearest court of admiralty. Although we declined bills for our prizes, the Portuguese authorities at Rio had no hesitation in taking our captain's bill upon the Transport Board in England. They relieved us from the charge of our prisoners, about 800 in number, and agreed to provide for them, and convey them in cartel to France, delivering them as British prisoners of war. The stipulated sum to be paid for the performance of this service was 10,000*l.* sterling.

Having completed our supplies of wood and water, and revelled for about three weeks in the productions of this luxurious land, where the oranges are, if possible, finer and more abundant than even in China, and having thus given a check to any incipient scurvy among our crew, we again set off upon our voyage, meaning to call at the Capoeof Good Hope, and leave our prizes there, being no longer encumbered with their French crews.

We stood to the southward to get into the westerly gales; but had hardly reached their confines when we met with a specimen of them that proved too severe a trial for one of the French ships: she sprang a-leak. We bore up, and were glad to get her in safety back to Rio Janeiro, and to accept the terms we had before declined, with this difference, that only three thousand, instead of seven, was given for the leaky ship and all her contents. The price of the other was not changed.

The prize-money I received for this capture, on our return to England a year and a half afterwards (about 150*l.*) was the largest sum I ever made in that way in the course of twenty-two years' service. During that time I was present at the taking of many of the enemy's vessels, chiefly men-of-war; and the whole of the sums of prize-money taken together, which fell to my share, was considerably under 400*l.* This amount I look upon to be a fair average of this source of emolument to naval officers of the rank I held during that busy time, namely, midshipman about seven years, and lieutenant about fifteen. I am particular in stating this, because the country is under a delusion as to the amount of advantage which naval officers derive from prize-money, by hearing of some lucky individuals, similar in number to those who gained prizes in the lottery.

Once more we set off with our convoy, and stood to the southward to get into "the gales that should drive us along," and saw no land from this time until we made the western coast of New Holland, a distance of about eight thousand miles. In a voyage to China, iltis not until this stage of it that one can enter with full zest into the spirit of the song which extols the charms of the"wide unbounded sea"-

" Without a mark, without a bound,
It runneth the earth's wide region round;
It plays with the clouds, it mocks the skies,
Or like a cradled infant lies."

This, with the sheer water and the soaring albatross, added to the author's accompaniments of "the blue above and the blue below," are all delightfully associated with the feeling of freedom and security which the sailor derives from the consciousness that there is not a rock within a thousand miles of him. But if they are pleasing to those whose "march is on the mountain wave, whose home is on the deep," I fear that to the mere passenger, it is only-by reminding him that this dreary stage of the voyage is over, that those objects can be agreeable.

In an Indiaman, when the passengers happen to be well assimilated, they have much social intercourse and amusement, enlivened by the presence of the fair sex, who rarely grace the decks of a man-of-war at sea; but all the agreeable varieties with which they are enabled to wile away the sense of their confinement, in crossing the fine-weather latitudes, must be sadly broken in upon, and those which depend upon the female part of their society entirely put aside, when the storm comes "to awake the deep," and they cannot say with its nursling, "No matter – I can ride and sleep."

In the line of this vast Southern Ocean, which ships bound to India or China traverse, to run down their easting, the changes of weather are frequent, but the order of those changes is less variable than what we meet with in corresponding latitudes in the Northern Atlantic. In the belt between the 38th and 42d degrees of south latitude, where the easting should be made, the period of a round of the weather which accompanies the wind in making a round of the compass, is frequently performed in forty-eight hours. Let us begin with a clear blue sky, the surface of the sea like "a cradled infant, "which fain would rest, but it cannot for the violent heaving of the ground-swell which the last westerly gale has left to roll on until it shall be again impelled forward by the next; while your ship, that with a breeze would "walk the waters like a thing of life," is now tossed and tumbled without control, and receives more damage in her sails and rigging than in a gale of wind. In such a case a careful officer will take in the sails that cannot be useful, and set them again when they can; and not in pure idleness leave them to be worn out by banging against the masts.

While your ship, deprived of her *vital* power is rolling awkwardly on the waves, the birds of the ocean are riding gracefully over them, now seated on the water, and resting from the labours of the storm, during which they had soared in the air with ceaseless wing.

When a few hours have tired you of this restless calm, light airs of wind from the eastward induce you again to make sail, more to steady your ship than to make any progress on your voyage. The wind blowing from the point you would steer upon, and so light that you can make but little way in any direction. You lie up about S.S.E., on the larboard tack; gradually the wind draws to the northward, and as it comes round to admit of your lying nearer and nearer to your couse, it freshens.

You come up to S.E. and to E.S.E., and now to steer east, with fore top-mast and top-gallant studding-sails set, while the tumbling swell of the last gale, still following, helps you onward. With the wind between N.N.E. and N., the sky begins to overcast, and some rain perhaps falls. The wind freshens, and you can no longer carry your royals and top-gallant studding-sails. You take them in, and you may send them down to the sail-room if they be dry, for you may depend upon it you will have a gale of wind before you want them again.

Soon you find the fore-top-mast studding-sail and top-gallant-sails too much; and when you take them in, and reef your topsails, down with the top-gallant yards and masts on deck; and now reef away, furl your fore and mizen topsails. The increase of the gale, as it draws from the westward of north, will keep pace with your exertions until you have her under a close-reefed main topsail and reefed foresail. By the time you have done this, you will find the wind at N. W., or more to the westward, and blowing a roaring gale-before which you may reel along, perhaps for a succession of several days, without any increase to this sail, if you do not sometimes find it too much for her. Your daily run during this kind of weather will probably vary between 230 and 250 *nautical* miles, or about an average of 280 *statute* miles. I once made a run, measured by chronometers, and difference of observed latitudes, of 263 nautical miles, or 304 statute miles, in 24 hours; and in the old B—, when running under the above reduced sail, I have the log, and repeated the operation when she was honestly going 13½ knots, or 15½ statute miles per hour.

The duration of these gales is by no means uniform. As I have said, they will sometimes carry you along for a succession of days, and sometimes the round of the weather is completed in forty-eight hours, or even less. When the wind draws from the southward of west, it begins to abate and the sky to clear. A short period of your run remains with moderate wind and a clear blue sky; but as the wind draws more to the southward, it dies away, and again leaves you to the rocking of a restless calm. The birds take to the water, and the round is completed.

The ornithology of the southern hemisphere – at least that of its ocean – appears to introduce you to another world of the feathered creation. This fact is, of course, known to naturalists, but I do not remember to have met with any remark upon it. The albatross and some varieties of the petral tribe, and, as you approach land, the penguins (if they may be called birds) are most apparent to the voyager who is not versed in natural history, as being wholly unlike anything he meets with in corresponding latitudes of the northern hemisphere. In the northern Atlantic, too, we look for the appearance of birds as indicating the approach to soundings; but in the Southern Ocean, we see the majestic albatross and some other birds thousands of miles from the nearest land, and this not casually or seldom, but continually.

The succession of weather I have described as prevailing with more uniformity in the belt of the Southern Ocean referred to, than in corresponding latitudes of the Northern Atlantic, may amuse the old voyager by the likeness of the picture, and may be useful to let the stranger in those seas know what he is to expect; but the true sailor, in adding to his knowledge the experience of others, will never trust to it so far as to lull his vigilance, and to supersede that 'good look-out' which old Nicholson quaintly classes as one of the three L's that a seaman must not lose sight of – *'lead, latitude, and look-out.'*

If he should trust implicitly to the uniform progress of the above round of weather, he may sometimes be astonished, and have his ship brought by the lee when steering east with a gale from the north-west by a thundering squall bursting upon his starboard quarter, with hardly the warning of a momentary lull; and if he be not quick in clapping his helm a-starboard, and bracing round his head-yards, the south-wester will broach him to, and send his masts over the side. In these sudden shifts of wind from N.W. to S.W. the first gust is often tremendous; but I do not recollect any instance of its blowing hard from the S.W. for any length of time in these latitudes. We had many a turn of the weather as above described before we hauled up to the northward, and made the north-west coast of New Holland –and a sterile and barren-looking coast it is. We saw no smoke, nor any other symptom of inhabitants, and but little verdure. That which might have been in a cooler season was now (in December) scorched by a vertical sun – which also gave us a good roasting after our refreshing sail in the Southern Ocean. Soon after we left this land, we were becalmed for several days; and I do not remember to have suffered so much from heat at any other time in the open sea. One of our men died from a coup-de-soleil, and two others, one a fine young fellow, went mad. At this time, too, we lost one of our primest men, the gunner's mate, who had saved the ship in the North Sea, by discovering that the gun-tackles had been cut. In the morning, about eight o'clock, we had spread the awnings, and prepared, as well as we could, for another burning day, when he was performing some trifling work outside of the hull of the ship, and, slipping his hold, fell overboard. He swam well, and endeavoured to catch hold of the ship as she glided past him, and of ropes that were thrown to him; but nobody seemed to be aware of the rate at which we were going, for although it was perfectly calm on deck, the lofty sails were filled with a light air of wind which was right aft; and we were sliding along at the rate of about three knots. It was not until he was astern that the helm was put down, and an endeavour made to clear the boat; but, in the boisterous weather we had been accustomed to encounter, the quarter- boats had been lashed and secured as if it were intended that they never should be lowered again. By the time she was ready for lowering, the man was a full cable's length on the weather-beam of the ship, which had been hove-to. He was still swimming, with hi shead well above water, and until now had been silent; but at this time he gave a piercing scream of despair, and we saw him no more. It was said that a shark must have seized him, as he disappeared so suddenly; but it is more probable that he had been taken with cramp, or his power of swimming bad been exhausted; for, although, when the boat arrived on the spot, too late to see anything of him, the people in hcr pickcd up his hat, they saw no traces of blood in the water, and had a shark taken him, the water would, probably, have been stained with it. In the only instance of this kind I ever witnessed, the water was covered with blood to a great extent. The loss of this poor man seemed to throw a gloom over us all: he was one of the best men in the ship; and although we had had some hair-breadth escapes, and broken up an enemy's squadron, he was the first man we had lost since we left England. The manner of his death, too, in a fine calm morning – illustrating the poet's conception of danger which "frowns in the storm, but in the sunshine strikes" – increased the feeling for him: at least, I know that I did not get his last and only scream out of my head for a long time. The con-verse of the poet's conception of danger, namely, its only frowning in the storm, every man who has been accustomed to brave it becomes familiar with; as also with the fact, that it looks much more formidable at a distance than when fairly encountered.

Long after the incident I have just related, I lent a hand to save the life of a man on whom the danger seemed to frown much more than on our poor friend, the gunner's mate. We were coming across the Atlantic in a 74 alone; it had been blowing a gale all night from the N.W. We were under a reefed foresail and close-reefed main topsail, top-gallant yards on deck, and top-gallant masts struck. During the morning watch, the gale increased so much that it was thought right to send the top-gallant masts on deck. I was first-lieutenant of the ship, and at seven bells (half-past seven) I took charge of the ship, and per- mitted the officer of the watch to go below to perform his toilet, and prepare for breakfast. When the masts were sent down, one of the fore-castle men, who had gone into the lee-fore-chains, to gather in the slack of the top-gallant back-stays, was washed out by a violent lurch of the ship ; and the "flying cords," torn from his grasp by the weather-roll, left him at the mercy of the "tumbling billows of the deep." He swam well, however, and buffeted them with lusty sinews. The main-hatchway-gratings happened to have been got up on the poop, for the purpose of stowing the hammocks upon them, which could not be kept in their accustomed place by reason of the roughness of the sea. On the impulse of the moment, one of those gratings was thrown overboard to the man. "Down with the helm!" – "Man the fore-clew-garnets!" – "Clear away the lee-quarter boat!" were orders soon given; and while the fore-sail was hauling up, and the boat being cleared away, I jumped into the cabin, to ask the Captain whether she should be lowered.

There are times in the open ocean when the attempt to despatch a boat from the ship would be attended with instant and certain death to all who should be sent in her. Short of this, there are times also when the prospect of such a result may make the question of, whether a boat shall be despatched, one of anxious consideration for the officer who is to give the answer; particularly if he himself is not to partake of the risk. Our Captain was placed in this situation; when, looking from the cabin windows, he saw the man reach the grating, and secure his floating by a good hold of it. This determined him. He answered, "Yes." When I got to the deck again, the boat was ready for lowering; but, as yet, there was nobody in her. In ordinary cases a four-oared boat would have been despatched from a seventy-four with a mid-shipman, or some officer of less consideration than a first-lieutenant; who, indeed, is never sent on business detached from the ship, except it be to attack an enemy. Here there was no time to be lost, and I felt that the onus rested on me to order men into the boat, or to show them the example by going myself. The last was the shortest mode, and the "come along" which accompanied my spring out of the mizen rigging, was answered by men crowding to follow. We did not want a crowd; and when the first four had got in, I ordered the rest back, and directed the men at the tackles to lower away.

The boat was a small one of four oars, built of very light wood, and had taken the place of a large heavy one, which had been damaged; so that the tackles were too large for her; and her weight was hardly sufficient to draw the rope through their pullies. The stern tackle was lowered more freely than the other; and the more the stern of the boat went down, the more the rope of the foremost tackle was jammed in the pullies by lying obliquely to their direction, so that it stuck fast. The roaring of the wind and sea made the orders given from the outside of the ship not easily heard; and our calling out to "hold fast the stern tackle,' was not attended to until the stern of the boat came bang down upon the sea with every lee-lurch, while her bow was still suspended by the foremost tackle, which could not be unhooked; and again, with the weather roll, we took a flying leap into the air, of twenty or thirty feet. We were retained in the performance of these involuntary vaultings until they had been several times repeated. I had hung the rudder, and held by the after tackle, in order to be in readiness to unhook it and throw it clear of the boat; but when it slackened, by her stem coming on the water, I luckily had presence of mind enough, before I did so, to look forward, in order to see if the fore tackle was ready to be unhooked at the same time; and as the boat was hung by it, to hold fast. Had I suffered the after tackle to be unhooked, we should have been swung into the air by the one tackle alone, and coming down with the lee-lurch right on end, we should have been dashed, not on the water, but into it. The remedy was at length perceived: a man was sent out on the david to overhaul the foremost tackle; we unhooked, and got clear of the ship.

We had nothing now but fair play, and a rough sea to encounter. To pull to windward was the least dangerous part of our task; and we rose over the precipitous waves that met us like a sea-gull. When we had worked at this for about a quarter of an hour, we began to fear that our labour was in vain. We had as yet seen nothing of the man; and now we supposed that we must have passed over the place where he had fallen, and that he had gone down. The men looked wistfully at the ship, which was driving fast to leeward. "Let us give way, and try to find the grating,-and then we shall be sure." They again plied their oars. In a high sea it is not easy for a person seated in a little boat to see anything floating, which does not rise much above the surface: in fact, it is physically impossible, except at such time as the boat and the object looked for happen to be each on the top of a wave at the same instant. From the top of one wave the surface of the water can only be seen between it and the next: the heads of the more remote, only show themselves on a level with the nearest ones. Thus we had as yet seen nothing of him, and had nearly given up the endeavour, when the happy coincidence of our rising to the top of a wave at the same time with him occurred. I *fancied* that I saw for an instant an erected arm, and called out to encourage the men. The next wave on which we rose removed all doubt, and showed us the man still boldly floating nearly breast high, supported by the grating, and not far from us. A little more rowing enabled us to reach him: the bowman laid in his oar, and pulled him on board. Having accomplished this, he laid hold of the grating to pull it in also. This operation appeared to add to the dangerous situation of the boat by pressing her bows down into waves over which she already seemed to rise as by a miracle. I therefore called out to the bowman to quit it, and resume his oar; but the man, with more coolness and more foresight than myself, remonstrated by saying, " t may be useful to us, sir." He was allowed to proceed, and followed up his precaution by putting the grating carefully under the thwarts, or seats, of the boat. It was lucky he did so; for the buoyant power of the grating thus placed, added to the lightness of the boat, made her a complete life-boat, and saved our lives.

Lord Byron observes, that a "tight boat will live in a rough sea;" and so she will, particularly when going with her bow to it. But it may prove too much for her, and is more likely to do so if following upon her quarter, as we now had it on our way back to the ship. The appearance of the waves as they curled over her, could hardly justify the hope of her surmounting them, as a black squall came on. After rising over many that appeared ready to swallow us, one fellow came, whose curving crest projected his head over us with all the gracefulness of a swan's neck. As the boat's stern rose erect on this wave, her head was pressed under the surface, and the wave impelling her forward, launched us under water while it rolled over us. At this moment several thoughts passed fleetly through my mind; the chief of which was, that the chance of meeting my friends again in this world was now up. We held instinctively to the boat, which came out on the other side of the wave, not keel up, as I should have expected: indeed, I cannot now understand how it was that the impelling power of the wave did not turn her over when it launched her under water head foremost. Out she came, however, on the other side of the wave, waddling like a duck. When we found that she was not to go down with us, we caught three out of the four oars; the other went astern with our hats and every loose thing in the boat. The lightness of the wood she was built of, and the buoyant principle of the grating, which now floated and pressed upwards against the thwarts, bore her up with her rollocks well out of the water; while, as she waddled from side to side, more of the water which was in her was thrown out. When I perceived this, I made the man whom we had saved, sit down in the bottom of the boat, with his head only above water, in order to his displacing his own bulk of it. He was a heavy man, and not now capable of much exertion. Two of the men whose hats were saved by being fastened with rope‑ yarns, were employed to bale with them. The other two got their oars out, while I resumed my place at the helm, and steered for the ship no longer, but directly before the sea, across her wake. For some time it seemed labour in vain; and once, when we had got the boat half baled out, another sea, without the ceremony of lifting us, as the former had done, rolled over us; but we had learned by this time, that all is not lost that is in danger; so we baled away again, and steered before the wind until we had got to leeward of the ship ; watched an opportunity to round to; and being now able to pull for her with the sea on our bow, we ultimately got safe on board.

CHAPTER XIII

WHILE upon the subject of narrow escapes in boats, I may mention another which arose from my own mismanagement or want of forethought, as it may possibly prevent some young officer from getting into a similar scrape. When I was Lieutenant of H.M.S. A—, cruizing off the coast of France, we were despatched in chase of an American merchant-ship, which appeared to have come out of a French port. This was during the existence of Bonaparte's Berlin and Milan Decrees, and our reciprocal Orders in Council, which endeavoured to put an end to all neutrality, by each of the great belligerent nations interdicting all the world from having intercourse with the other.

Bonaparte's power was great; but the edicts of a despot, and even of one who has had talent to make himself such, cannot be enforced over a wide extent of country in opposition to the habits and interests of the people. Bonaparte failed to exclude the productions of Great Britain and her colonies from the Continent. The complicated nature of British commerce soon made it necessary for her government to. relax its Orders in Council, by granting licenses for neutral vessels to enter the ports of France; and such licenses, being easily forged, were manufactured and sold at a cheap rate; but vessels trading by them were obliged to conceal the fact of their having them from the French authorities. They also had a great objection to being boarded by a British man-of-war upon the high seas; for such communication was, by an edict of Bonaparte's, made equivalent to their having been in a British port, and subjected them to condemnation if they afterwards came into a French one.

When we started in chase of this suspicious vessel, we had a moderate breeze, and a fine blue sky, the wind about south. It was a favourite maxim of a much-respected commander with whom I once sailed, that we should "never trust a Frenchman or a southerly wind," and so it turned out. The sky soon overcast, and the wind increased to a gale. The chase was on our weather-bow, and made all sail from us. She sailed well for a merchant-ship, but was light, and soon lost her advantage of being to windward. We got her under our lee-bow and carried our foretop-mast studding-sail until it was blown away. For a while we carried the maintop-gallant sail over double-reefed topsails, but were forced to take it in : however, as we could now round in our weather- braces by reeving preventer ones and settling the topsail haulyards, we continued to carry this sail over the courses with the jib well eased in on the boom, and kicked up a furious foam as we ploughed through it. Our cross-jack yard not being supported by braces, went off into three pieces, and sent the fragments of the mizen-topsail clattering about our ears until we got it taken in. Our chase carried sail well too; but it now became too much for her, and besides, she saw that we were gaining ground upon her fast, so she took all in but a close-reefed maintop sail. Our ship was well manned; so having close reefed the topsails, the watch was left to take in further sail as we neared her. It happened to be my watch on deck; and when we had taken in the foretop sail and were running down under the maintop sail and foretop-mast stay-sail, orders were given to clear away the boat. This reminded me that if she were despatched during my watch it would be my duty to go in her. I had been out in rougher weather; but the business of facing it now was not a pleasant one: the sea was running high, and there was no excitement in the prospect of boarding a light merchant-ship that we well knew would have a licence, whether real or fictitious. Before we were near enough to round to and lower the boat, the watch drew very near to a close. We are not always in the humour for enterprize, and although I was ready enough to have gone in the boat with a good grace while it was my turn for duty, I felt at this moment an unworthy anxiety to hear the bell strike that should call up my relief. When we were about to round to, the end of the watch was reported, and the bell was struck as the helm was put down. I was prepared to let the boat be lowered and hauled up alongside for her officer in due form. – "S— will be in no hurry with his relief," thoughtI , – but I was mistaken. Before the sound was out of the bell he appeared. The sight of his bat as it ascended above the deck with the last stroke of the bell turned the tide of all the illiberal calculations of the last five minutes; so I pocketed the boarding-book, and nodding to my friend S— to take charge of the ship, jumped into the boat and was lowered down in her with the crew, instead of waiting for her to be hauled up for me, notwithstanding the remonstrances of S—, who claimed the duty as his.

We got alongside of the American ship, and jumping on her deck with a lee-lurch, I was soon satisfied that she had one of the licences above-mentioned ; so, noting her name, &c. in the boarding-book, I returned to the boat and ordered the bow-man to shove off, the men llaving their oars in perfect readiness. But here is the point in which I was wrong, and to which I would call the attention of young officers. The ship was so light, and driving so fast to leeward, that we could not get free from her side to make the oars effectual, until by her drawing a-head we came under her counter, which fell upon us with the send of the ship, and would infallibly have sent us under water if the gunnel-streak of the boat had not given way. Before the stern of the ship fell a second time, she was far enough a-head to be clear of us, but barely so, and her counter grazed our stem as she fell. Had I done what was right, and looked about me before I returned to the boat, I should have directed the master of the ship to hoist his fore-staysail and put his helm a-weather, until the ship, and therefore the boat alongside of her, had steerage-way; and then jumping into the boat, given her a broad sheer off before we slipped the rope that held her. Had I done so we should have dropped astern, clear of the ship without any trouble. As it was, I was more fortunate than I deserved to be. We got back to H.M.S. without further damage. Our summer gale broke up, according to the beautifully descriptive line of Tommy Moore, "A beam of tranquility smiled in the west." We made sail and rejoined the fleet. But this is some years in advance of the voyage with which we were going on.

Having got into the lazy latitudes again, our progress was slow, and a good many days passed in the calm and hot weather before we made the Island of Sandal-wood, and at last anchored in the Strait of Sapi, at the east end of the Island of Sumbawa. The first day was spent in trying to open some negociation with the natives. A captain oft he Indiamen who had been in these seas before, undertook this diplomatic mission. The chief declined to give any formal permission for our being supplied, from a fear of the Dutch at some factory in the neighbourhood who had assumed an authority over them;

but we afterwards found the people inoffensive, and ready to sell us turtle, buffaloes, live stock, and vegetables for ringas (dollars), of which they perfectly understood the use. When the news of our arrival spread abroad over the island, and it was known that there was a ready demand and good payment for those articles, they became abundant; but for the first day or two there was but little prospect of our being able to obtain any supply beyond that of wood and water. On the first day none of the natives came near us. The captain of the Indiamnn who had gone on shore, happened to be a sportsman, and knew what he should meet with, so having taken a fowling-piece with him, he bagged a lot of pheasants, and brought a leash of them to our captain when he returned. This was the only fresh meat in our ship this day excepting that in the cock-pit. The midshipmen of the starboard berth 11ad preserved the little pig which they were allowed to take on board at Rio Janeiro, so that, when we made the land on the evening before, he had become a very respectable porker, and died the usual death of a pig. His fry with a lot of chops had given us a sumptuous breakfast; his head manufactured into mock-turtle soup, his two legs roasted, one fore-quarter boiled, and the other made into a pie, afforded a grand dinner, of which the larboard berth were invited to partake, and a favourite lieutunant (old Stoyle), and the doctor honoured us with their company. The youngsters whose turn it was to dine in the cabin and in the wardroom were in tribulation at the sight of the captain's or the wardroom steward, lest they should come to deliver the usual message. With the wardroom this point was easily settled, but to decline dining in the cabin was a much more formidable matter: the one to whom this lot fell was not a favourite with us, still we were sorry for him, and laid our heads together to get him off; we had settled our plan of operations by speaking to our favourite lieutenant, who undertook to make his excuse to the captain. when the young gourmand got a sight of the pheasants, he changed his mind, and left us to enjoy this "one long day of revelry and ease" without his company, which we voted to be no loss. Four o'clock of the next morning called us to commence the fagging work of wooding and watering. A small rivulet flowed through the *jungle* into the sea opposite to our anchorage; but this place was not sufficiently advanced within the strait lo be entirely protected from the swell of the Southern Ocean, that found its way in and made a bad surf over some rocks and shallow water which here extended from the shore, and caused our intercourse with it by boats to be difficult and dangerous at the time of ebb tide; so we had trouble enough until we became acquainted with the local circumstances, of which we were able afterwards to take advantage, and thereby to manage matters better.

Of the incidents of our youth to which we have pleasure in reverting, there are none, excepting such as remind us of the sacrifice of selfish feelings in a virtuous cause, to which we look back with more complacency than the feats of exertion or endurance we could then undergo with impunity, but which, at an advanced age, we feel our bodily frame to be no longer fitted for. On one of our early days at the above work, I had been sent in charge of a watering party at four o'clock in the morning; the boats were despatched to the ships with a load; they were to return for another after getting their breakfast, and to bring ours with them; we, in the mean time, were employed in filling and rolling down the casks which they were to take off at nine o'clock. It may be believed the watering party were ready for their breakfast, and therefore looked anxiously for the return of the boats which came about this time; when they arrived, sundry tin pots of cocoa and parcels of biscuit made their appearance for the men – *mine was to come in the next boat.* The men would readily have given me a part of theirs, but I trusted to the arrival of my own; the next boat was sent about something else, and did not come for water. Working with my men between the boats and the confluence of the stream, through an ugly surf and over a burning sand, I was glad when we got them loaded and despatched to the ship, in hopes of their returning and not forgetting my dinner, or breakfast – for I felt as if I could eat both. I often cast a wistful eye to the ship to see them shove off; but as the tide had ebbed, the surf was judged to be too much for them, and they did not return until a late hour in the evening, when they came to take us off. It was therefore not thought worth while to bring our provisions. We arrived on hoard about eight o'clock. Although by mismanagement nothing had been sent to me, so that I had been without food the whole day, yet I found that my breakfast and dinner, and something more than my allowance of grog, had been carefully put by for me. I made up for lost time by discussing the whole of these articles at one meal; nor was this a very difficult task. The length of our eastern passage, and the prospect of that part of it which still lay before us, had made it necessary to put us on half allowance of salt beef, and the farinaceous part of our diet, such as bread, &c., to which a youngster in health trusted for filling his stomach, was reduced in allowance also; but what remained made up in quality for its deficiency in quantity: you might have blown a biscuit into the maintop; no puff-paste ever excelled it in lightness, although the process which effected the same excellence in both was different. The biscuit was enriched with the living and dead carcases of succeeding races of *bargemen* (black- headed maggots) and of some hundred generations of weevils, which presented no bill of mortality; and the esteemed character of lightness was produced by the solid contents of the biscuit being reduced to the state of honeycomb, and the interstices filled with a powder which had been sublimed in its passage through these animals; the larger cavities were filled with cobwebs, which marked the place of sepulture of the departed generations of bargemen, and served for their winding-sheets, though these mausoleums were sometimes disturbed by the restless spirit of a young race of centipedes. To make up for the light quality of the biscuit, the *doughboy* which accompanied my piece of salt beef, though small, was heavy enough. Having made my meal and applied the liberal allowance of grog that had been provided for me, to reduce the discordant elements to a due state of amalgamation, I was ready for rest. My hammock was hung over the cable-tier, the usual dormitory of midshipmen, which is the most comfortable quarter the ship during a gale of wind in the north sea; but under present circumstances, the prospect of going clown there to be stewed, after the roasting I had had during the day, was not agreeable, and the insidiously cool land wind already came invitingly into the gun-room stern-ports, which were open. So taking advantage of a large chest that happened to be near them, I stretched myself upon it, with my jacket under my head for a pillow, and was soon in a sound sleep. About two o'clock, I dreamed that I was overboard, and awoke in a cold shivering fit. I recollected all the good advice that the doctor had given us, "not to sleep exposed to the land-wind," and fancied that I was fairly in for all the evils which he had predicted as the consequence of this exposure; so I was glad now to partake of the stewing which I had avoided in the evening, and making off to my hammock, I rolled myself in a blanket, again fell asleep, and felt no more of the illness which I had thus been warned of by the premonitory symptoms. Nevertheless I would recommend all youngsters who are disposed to take advice, to "mind what the doctor says."

To assist us with our wooding and watering, one of our convoy that had some repairs to make, which employed all his hands, delayed his business of watering until the other work should be completed, and having therefore no use for his long-boat, lent it to us. She was manned with a crew of our own hands, and I had now the separate charge of her assigned to me. When we had completed the watering of our ship, the same crew were employed in her to expedite the supplying of the one to which she belonged; and on this service my men as well as myself lived in clover: for besides the shortened allowance of his Majesty on board our own ship, which was reserved for our return to her in the evening, our meals were always ready for us on board the Indiaman, to prevent the delay of going for them, and I was furnished with a supply of spirits, to give to the men at my discretion. Our duties being uninterrupted by anything else that was going on, I, for the first time in my life, felt the independence of being a commanding officer; and the power I held in my hands, by the control over this extra allowance of spirits, was sufficient to keep my men in prime working order, without any appeals or complaints, so they were no less eager than myself to cut out the boats of the Indiamen by bringing off more turns of water. I had now an opportunity of ascertaining how much time is requisite for a party of men to get their dinners and be again on duty, when everything is properly arranged for them, and when the spirit of the men is engaged in their work. We arrived on board one day with a load at twelve o'clock; the hands were upon deck ready to hoist it in;

the chief-mate, who met me as I came up the side, informed me that dinner was ready for my men, and begged me to call them up, while he sent his own hands to sling the casks. I told my men to get their dinners and return to the boat as fast as they could, without waiting to be called up. Upon my saying this, the chief-mate looked at his watch: before the last cask was out of the boat, my men appeared on the gangway. When they had all got into the boat, tossed their oars up, and were ready to shove off, as I was about to go over the side, the officer of the Indiaman again looked at his watch and said, "Your men have been just ten minutes, Sir." Ten minutes was a short time for seventeen men to have despatched their dinner, and to be again on duty; but they had not much carving to interrupt them : their meal was of turtle-soup put out into vessels for them, and by the care of their good caterer, already sufficiently cooled to allow them to bale away.

Our intercourse with the shore now became more interesting by communication with the natives, who formed a market under a range of cocoa-nut trees near the beach, and supplied us abundantly with vegetables and poultry. Most of us retained some relic of the French frigates we had taken; this, though not regular, it was very customary to do. I had got hold of one of those fowling-pieces that our Guinea-men were in the habit of carrying as a part of their cargo to barter for slaves, and which the Frenchmen had taken. When our wooding and watering were completed, and while we yet waited for some of the most tardy ships, some of us got permission to have a ramble on shore; and by way of *resting* after our fatigues, passed a long day in wandering through the jungle in quest of game, which, having fed in the cool of the morning, were too wise to expose themselves to any exertion under the rays of a burning sun, where the thermometer stood at 120° Fahr. : accordingly we had but little sport. It appeared to be known to the natives that this was to be the last day of our stay among them, and the market-place was considerably enlarged and well supplied. When the party of sportsmen returned in the evening – who, by the bye, had only the one fowling-piece among them, we found quantities of fowl and vegetables, which yet remained to be disposed of. Our frolic in the shooting excursion had been planned ever since the appearance of the pheasants, and had been a subject of much interest among us; but as that was completed, and moreover as it had failed to obtain for us the anticipated abundance of game, I thought the best thing I could now do with the fowling-piece was to make it available for providing our mess in another manner. We exchanged it with the native for six dozen fowls, and as many pumpkins, yams, and sweet potatoes, as we could carry down the beach while the boat was coming on shore for us.

Next morning we weighed and began to make our way through that chain of fine-weather sailing among the numerous islands that divide the seas in this quarter into a labyrinth of straits, from which the swell of the ocean is cut off. The sea is therefore always smooth, and as the weather is always fine, navigation here would form the very beau ideal of a fresh-water sailor's paradise, but that the zephyrs which fan him nurse in their soft breath seeds of disease and death, which Boreas, where he prevails, disperses, although his manners are not so gentle-manlike.

And now commenced the melancholy process that cut down the flower of our gallant crew. When this happens in action it is what is looked for, and the survivors have the satisfaction of paying a tribute to their departed companions in the remembrance of their heroic deeds; but when "the pestilence that walketh in darkness," and " the destruction that wasteth at noonday," steal silently onward among your men, until gaining more and more strength, they make rapid havoc on every side; when each day brings a succession of sufferers, supported by their messmates to meet your morning visit, who were yesterday full of life and spirit, and who to-morrow send forth their groans from a painful death-bed, – this is indeed a melancholy and a trying time.

I believe it is a fact recognized in the army, as well aa in the navy, that 1t 1s not while men are engaged in extraordinary exertion and exposure that they are liable to be cut down by sickness, but that the reaction which takes place during the comparative rest that follows, the penalties of the exposure are suffered.

Taking on board the fuel and water of a man-of-war, even when it is brought off to her, is no light work for her crew, as the quantity required must fill her capacious bulk, and is to her what a cargo is to a merchant-ship. But when the wood is to be cut down in a tropical jungle, and to be got off, as well as the water-casks to her boats, over a burning sand and through a rolling surf, her men and officers are necessarily exposed to an arduous and trying species of fatigue. It was after being thus employed that our men showed symptoms of the disease that was in our return voyage to commit such sad havoc; but when we were again in the open ocean, and more particularly when we had ceased to use for drinking the water that had been put into empty spirit and wine casks, the disorder abated; and after our arrival at Macao, the cool air and the plentiful supplies of fresh meat restored those invalids who had survived.

In the West Indies fever is the general consequence of exposure and exertion; but among these islands the prevailing disease is dysentery. The cause of this difference would be an interesting, and perhaps, useful subject of inquiry for the physiologist. But I am satisfied that one means of promoting dysentery, is prevented by the use of iron tanks in the navy, in lieu of water-casks.

Long after this time I was ordered to proceed from India to China, during the season when the N.E. monsoon, blowing down the China sea, makes it necessary to take the long, or eastern route. I had orders also to visit Amboyna. The ship I then commanded had been recently fitted at Bombay, and was there supplied with a set of water- casks. To preserve these casks from becoming leaky by drying up while in store, they had been filled with water which was at first not very choice, but which had become putrid; and by its having remained long in them, had thoroughly impregnated the casks with its offensive and injurious qualities. Three times in the course of about six weeks, we had started all the water on board, in order to have it renewed in them; but they still continued to impart to it their horrible taste and smell. The orders to proceed on this voyage did not require any great urgency of despatch beyond "convenient speed." So when I had got fairly over to Prince of Wales's Island, and out of the way of being interrupted in my progress, recollecting what the crew of the B— had suffered, and recognizing the stench of the water on board of her, as at least an aggravating cause, I determined to endeavour to prevent its existence the the ship I commanded, where some cases of dysentery had already proved fatal; and therefore erected a tent on shore, for a good cooper and a party of men to assist him ; and landing all the water-casks, I had every one of them opened, and burned out. I took care to supervise the work myself, so as to see that the whole of their inner surface was effectually *charred*. This occupied ten days, and of course delayed our voyage so much; but I thought myself amply repaid by having sweet and wholesome water for the crew during the whole of it; and although we had a good many cases of dysentery, in the course of eight months' navigation among those islands, we had none that proved fatal after the casks had been thus purified.

While threading our way through this archipelago in the B—., we saw none of the natives after we left the island of Sumbawa; but in the voyage I have just referred to, they came off to visit us in a remote and less frequented part than any we now explored. We then made our way into the Pacific Ocean, through Dampier's Strait, instead of the Gitola passage, which we followed in the B—. Dampier's Strait is formed by an island called Waygiow to the north, and by the island of Papua (the N.W. corner of New Guinea) on the south. Soon after daylight we saw some canoes coming off to us from the island of Waygiow. We found that their object was barter. They brought off, for this purpose, bananas, yams, and a few shells. There was, indeed, but a "beggarly account" of these articles; but in a part so little frequented, we were surprised to find them come off to us at all ; and treated the first party that honoured us with their company very liberally, supplying them with biscuit and rum. We soon found, however, that there was not any shyness among them which required this encouragment. We bad but little wind, going about two knots; and in a short time after the arrival of the first canoe, they came off to us from all directions, and we were surrounded with them in great numbers. I had allowed the men from the first three or four canoes to come freely on board; this they did with the activity of monkeys. They made no choice of the accommodation which the gangways afforded to come up the side; but wherever they could lay hold, ascended with the facility of those animals.

Their activity and importunity soon became troublesome; and as there appeared to be no end to their increasing numbers, I thought it a wise precaution to beat to quarters, to form the small-arm men on the quarter-deck, to make the seamen buckle on their cutlasses, and to remain thus armed while they carried on their barter.

These active savages were of an athletic form, and were remarkable in differing from the islanders more to the westward, in having curly hair. It is probably this circumstance that has given the name of New Guinea to their land, although their hair is not so woolly as that of the African negro. They appeared to have very little notion of the value of money. In one of the canoes under the stern, I saw a very fine shell, and I held out two or three dollars in offer for it, without effect. One of the seamen observing this, offered an old clasp-knife for it, which was readily accepted. The man brought the shell to me, and I gave him the dollars to spend where they would be more valued.

I felt much satisfaction in the recollection of having armed my men, as above-mentioned, when I heard, not long afterwards, of an attack being made upon a Southsea whaler, by a party of natives who came off to her from the Pellew islands. It is true that I was in a man-of-war, but if we had neglected the means which this put in my power, the name of a man-of-war would not have availed us much, and we should, probably, have invited an attack, the issue of which might have been very doubtful, if we had been off our guard; and if these savages had courage bearing any proportion to their strength and activity. Their numbers around the ship at one time could not have been less than three hundred, and their activity would have enabled them all to assemble on the deck of the ships within fifteen seconds of a given signal, if they had been encouraged by our remissness. They had with them spears, and bows and arrows, and some of them wore daggera resembling the Malay Kris.

The Southsea-man was saved by the whale-knives accidentally lying within reach of her crew; unknown to the natives, who made the attack. Their first blow was made at the captain, who actively avoided it, and called on his men to save themselves. It was fortunately in their power to do so, but not without a desperate struggle, in which several men were hurt, and I think one or two killed, before their assailants jumped overboard, like water dogs, took to their canoes, and made off.

"Never hold an enemy too cheap," is an old and an excellent maxim, whiich I was long in the habit of hearing repeated by one of the best and bravest of British admirals. Applied to the case in point, it may he altered to the following, viz.:– "Never consider your force to be such, that its name will protect you from an enterprising enemy, if you neglect to keep it in readiness for action."

I believe the opening into the Pacific Ocean, called Dampier's Strait, has been but little followed since that enterprising navigator gave his name to it. Having made this passage, as well as one more to the northward, I should say by the comparison, that in future I would avoid Dampier's Strait. The eastern end of the island of Waygiow terminates the land on the northern side of this strait, so that, as you leave it, you are exposed to the swell from the Pacific Ocean, which is here but ill named; while the northern coast of Papua continues to stretch itself beneath your lee to the E.N.E., and presents a most inhospitable aspect. As far as we could see, the iron-bound ,outline was only varied by precipitous and pointed rocks projecting from it. The wind is said to prevail from the northward here, and we had a strong indication of this prevalence by the high swell which rolled from that quarter, and exhausted itself in a line of breakers along that rugged strand. With it beneath your lee, it is impossible not to feel, that if a ship were caught here by a series of calm weather, or baffling winds, she might be thrown by the swell upon this dreary coast. When we got out of the strait and encountered this swell, we had a moderate breeze from the westward, which enabled us to haul up, so as to make an offing from this ugly line of breakers; but in doing this, we had a narrow escape from being wrecked upon an unknown shoal, which stood isolated in the open ocean.

Having entered the strait in the night, I had not· been in bed; so when we were fairly out, and had shaped a course with our fair wind, after breakfast I stretched myself upon a sofa to have some sleep. I had not long lain down, when I found the rolling of the ship become very heavy; but I fancied that it was only my having been accustomed to smooth water among the islands, that made me more sensible to it. I could not rest, however, and went upon deck to look about me. As I leaned over the gangway I could see some large fish swimming along, and regarding them more attentively, I could perceive that they were gliding over a bottom of coral rocks. Looking ahead, I observed the water to be discoloured, and most so on the larboard bow. "Hard a-port"- " Hands, trim sails " – were orders given, barely in time to save the ship. The first cast of the lead showed fourteen fathoms, and as we hauled off to the southward, we were able to weather, by a short distance only, rocks which appeared to rise nearly to the surface, whilst the depth of water on those we were passing over, was shown by the lead to be reduced to five fathoms. The ship drew nearly three fathoms, and one touch, with the swell that was running, would have sent us all to feed the fish. I gave the particulars of this shoal to the Admiralty; and I believe it is now inserted in their charts.

NOTICE OF THE LATE CAPTAIN ROBERT CAMPBELL, R.N,

WE regret exceedingly to have to report the death of this excellent officer; and, we grieve to add, one of our most interesting contributors. His friends authorise us to mention, that Captain Campbell was the author of the series of papers which have appeared in this journal under the title of "Recollections of a Sea-Life, by a Midshipman of the last century;" and we are satisfied, that no person could have perused the articles in question, without feeling that they were in the hands of an officer of talent and experience, and one possessed of excellent taste, judgment, and right feeling in all matters, private or professional. On public grounds, therefore, as well as the more selfish ones connected with the loss of an able assistant in our task, we sincerely regret the death of this officer, and we have no doubt that in this sentiment we shall be joined by many of our readers.

As we had not opportunities of knowing much of the private life of our late valued contributor, we applied to Captain Basil Hall, who first introduced him to us, and at whose instance he undertook to write the series of papers alluded to; and as Captain Hall is an old shipmate and friend of his, we cannot do better than insert the following letter, which we received in answer to our application :-

" United Service Club, 22nd January, 1833.

" Mr. Editor: I should most willingly give you such a sketch of my excellent friend, Captain Campbell's professional career as you ask for, did I not think that he has himself already executed this task much better than any one can do it for him. His memory is very safe in his own hands; for I feel well assured that no one can read the papers published by him in your Journal, under the title of Recollections of a Sea-Life, without sincerely respecting the author, and becoming insensibly attached to him. In truth, he was one of the best officers I have ever sailed in companionship with, and so thoroughly right-minded and right-hearted in all he thought, said, and did, that be won the confidence of all whose duty it was to act over him, or with him, or under him. I shall merely mention that he served for a considerable time as Sir Samuel Hood's first-lieutenant, and he enjoyed the hearty good opinion of that great judge of an officer's character.

" I feel strongly tempted to give you some anecdotes of my late friend's professional as well as his private life; but I check myself, from the fear that I may mistake my own private regard for the interest which your readers feel on the occasion. When a man has long lived in the eye of the public, and claimed their attention by important services, every one feels interested in knowing even the minutest details of his life. But when an officer's merits, however great they may be, and however valuable they might prove, if they had met with opportunities of distinction, are known only to his private friends, it is not, perhaps, the best way to augment his reputation, to detail such particulars as can find no ready sympathy with general readers. The following anecdote, however, is so striking in itself, and so characteristic of my poor friend, that I venture to send it you.

"In the year 1818, Captain Campbell was appointed to the command of the island of Ascension, which, it will be remembered, had been occupied by us during Buonaparte's detention at St. Helena. I forget what ship be was appointed to; which, however, he was to fit out in the river, for the purpose of carrying out his garrison and stores. Within a day or two after receiving his appointment, and while he was making preparations to leave home, a horse kicked him and broke his leg severely. Nevertheless, he had no thought of relinquishing his command, and the Lords of the Admiralty having kindly allowed his brother Captain Lewis Campbell to fit out the ship, he remained quietly in the country to recover. In five weeks afterwards, although he could not stand, as the bone had not united, he insisted upon having a cot contrived so as to hang up in the stage-coach, and in this way he came to London, and took up lodging close to the Admiralty. The fracture, which was found as bad or worse than before, was put to right in town, and he was desired to keep quiet. This injunction, however, was beyond his powers; and within a day or two he rose from his bed, and, with his leg actually dangling about, in spite of numerous splints and bandage, he proceeded to the Admiralty, and was admitted to a personal interview. His great anxiety was to know distinctly what was expected of him in his novel command; and as he felt that he could not gain this knowledge except by personal communication, he incurred the risk of protracting his cure rather than leave England uninformed of his duty. Accordingly it was not till several weeks after reaching Ascension that the bones of his leg began to knit, and long afterwards before he gained adequate strength to put in execution the purpose he had long projected of surveying the island. On the death of Buonaparte he was relieved from the command of Ascension. A geographical and geological account of Ascension was printed by Capt. Campbell in 1824, in Professor Jameson's Philosophical Journal – and I need not refer again to the papers in your Journal – only one of which, however, on manning the Navy (No. 41), bears his name.

"Among the papers of my friend there have been found many incipient articles which would have done credit to the pages of the United Service Journal, had he lived to have matured them. I venture to send you one of those which contains several characteristic touches, independently of being not a little interesting in itself.

" I remain, your most obedient servant,
" BASIL HALL."

"In the service of his country there are many trying situations in which an officer who devotes himself to it is liable to be placed. When these circumstances involve an equal participation of personal danger the die is soon cast, and the decision to be made is relieved from a load of that responsibility which must ever influence the feelings of a conscientious man, when he is called upon to sacrifice the lives of his fellow-creatures, without partaking an equal risk.

"In the case, for instance, of boats being despatched to attack an enemy when the commanding officer does not leave his ship to accompany them,– which, in general, he ought not to do, – all that an officer can do, in such circumstance, is to consider well the practicability of the service, and to exert his judgment in the preliminary arrangements which lie within his power – giving to his men credit for that courage, and to his officers credit for that courage and judgment and foresight, with which much is practicable that might be deemed impossible by the cool calculator.

"Having made his mind up, he must free himself from the trammels of that feeling of responsibility which has a tendency to damp the fire of all spirit of enterprise, and which, I would trust and believe, has been the cause of the instances we have heard of, where commanding officers have been censured for not bringing an enemy to action, rather than from any fear of personal danger.

"But whatever personal bravery a man may have, if he be troubled with this diseased degree of conscientiousness –this fear of responsibility, it must, as far as it goes, unfit him for the duties of an officer, but more particularly for those of a commanding officer.

:Supposing such un officer to be totally regardless of personal safety when put in competition with his duty, still cases will and do arise to every man who devotes his life to the service, which will put to a severe test that kind of resolution, the want of which I have noticed. There are some puzzling questions for a man who is liable to be influenced by this over-degree of conscientiousness, which he should turn in his mind, so as to be able to act upon when such cases occur to him.

"For instance – you are in chase of an enemy's man-of-war – you are coming up with her, but have no time to lose –her port is a-head – one of your men falls overboard – the life-buoy is cut adrift, as a matter of course, by somebody near it –you see the man swim well and get hold of it – yet if you shorten sail your chase gets off – what will you do?

"There can be no question of what would be the line of duty for an officer placed in such circumstances, yet it would be a severe trial for a brave and humane man."

EXTRACT FROM SIR BASIL HUNT'S INTRODUCTORY LETTER FOR MRS. CAMPBELL'S TALES ABOUT WALES

As our interest in the perusal of almost any book is much modified by our knowledge of the author, either personal, or through the medium of his former works ; and, as, at all events, a considerable portion of my pleasure in the first perusal of this volume arose from my friendship for the author's late husband, in companionship with whom it was written, I may perhaps excite some degree of the same sort of attention for it by telling who and what he was.

Captain ROBERT CAMPBELL, of the navy, had the honour of being a near relation – first cousin – of the great poet of that name[1]; and he enjoyed the still higher honour of his cordial and uninterrupted friendship to the day of his death.

When I first became acquainted with him, he was senior lieutenant of Sir Samuel Hood's flag ship, of which I was fifth lieutenant; and I was not less surprised to find a man of high scientific, literary, and professional attainments, in such a situation, than to discover that his great merits were scarcely, if at all, recognised by those about him. Nor, I suspect, was he fully aware of them himself, till the respect which I felt and at once freely avowed, by engaging the attention of his other brother officers, eventually placed him in a more fitting position than he had previously occupied in their esteem. Had we not shortly afterwards, as he humourously expressed it, "been plunged in peace," – an event which, however beneficial to the country at large, extinguished so many brilliant lights in the army and navy, – I have no doubt that my highly gifted friend would soon have been as much admired by the public as he was esteemed by those who had the pleasure and advantage of his acquaintance.

I shall here relate an anecdote illustrative of the spirit of the man, by which those who are best acquainted with the stuff of which an officer ought to be made, will readily understand

---

[1] *Thomas Campbell.*

176

how, with due encouragement and opportunity, and under the glorious excitement of war, he might have done the State some service.

When Napoleon was sent to St. Helena, it was thought prudent by the Government to occupy the island of Ascension, which lies also in the S. E. trade wind, and might perhaps have been used by those persons, who, it was well known, projected the escape of the Ex-Emperor. It was arranged that the island should be placed under a naval officer, with a proper crew of seamen and marines; and my friend, whose merits had been brought under the favourable notice of Lord Melville, then first Lord of the Admiralty, was selected for this command, and appointed to a ship, which was to carry out his crew and the necessary stores. Before hoisting his pendant, however, he obtained leave to run down to the country to make some domestic arrangements; but, when there, he received a kick from a horse, which broke his leg, and, of course, laid him on his beam ends. The fracture was so severe, that many officers would have considered such a mishap as a complete stopper to the voyage; but he, never dreaming of such a thing, wrote instantly to the Admiralty to mention the accident, and to request their Lordships to have the goodness to allow his brother, (an active and intelligent officer,) to fit out the ship, — in the hopes that, by the time the vessel was ready to sail, her commander would also be ready to get under weigh.

Their Lordships, anxious not to lose the services of the best possible person for the command in view, readily agreed to the proposal, and the ship was commissioned accordingly. But when the period arrived for despatching her, my poor friend's leg, of which both bones were shattered, was nearly as ill as on the day of the accident; for the process of knitting, as it is called, had not advanced beyond the first stages.

Of course his friends, backed by the doctors, declared it to be impossible that. he could move. "Not move !" he exclaimed, "do you think 1 have been lying on my back for five weeks without contriving something to meet this occasion? Pray send the Guard of the Tally Ho day-coach to me, and let us see if we cannot rig up an affair to take me to town!"

He had previously written to his brother to send him a sea cot, which, by the help of the guard, was placed inside the coach, and so suspended and guyed, that it struck against neither the sides nor the ends. When all was ready, he made himself be laid on a plank, and lifted in at the coach window, and then, as he styled it, he was "slewed fore and aft," and placed in the cot!

On reaching London he was lifted out at the Salopian, coffee-house, and having seen his brother, and made himself thoroughly acquainted with the state and condition of his ship, he declared his intention of going to the Admiralty to receive his orders in person. Remonstrance was in vain, and the doctor having, by his directions, clapped an "extra fish on his broken spar," he was once more lifted out and carried to our great nautical head quarters. There he raised himself on crutches, and actually managed to find his way up stairs, and to have an interview with Sir George Cockburn, during which his leg literally dangled about, as he expressed it, like a half-second's pendulum!

This degree of energy was not lost on the amiable and experienced officer, to see whom was the object he had in view in making this effort; and, as I said before, had the war continued – or rather been renewed – a more extended field for the exercise of his talents and spirit would undoubtedly have been afforded him. As it was, he carried out his ship, took command of his desert island, and some time after, when the bones were readjusted, he found leisure to make a geographical and geological survey of Ascension, an account of which appeared in the Edinburgh Philosophical Journal for January 1826. The chart constructed at the same time by him is now issued by the Hydrographical Office to Her Majesty's Ships on that station. He retained the command, with the entire satisfaction of his employers, till Bonaparte's death broke up, or rather changed, the nature of the establishment at Ascension.

Captain Campbell's energies having now nothing specifically professional to occupy them, took the useful turn of naval literature, and he published in the United Service Journal a series of admirable papers, entitled "Recollections of a Sea Life by a Midshipman of the last Century," in which he describes many parts of his own nautical life with a graphic force rarely equalled. He also printed several other valuable papers, particularly one on Manning the Navy in War, in No. 41 of that admirable professional periodical.

How much the present work owes to the companionship of such a man, I do not exactly know, nor, probably, could the author herself determine ; but I have been much pleased by recognising in it many of my late friend's opinions and sentiments, which, I need scarcely say, always took the direction of true honour, and breathed that generous, manly, and, above all, that cheerfull spirit, which it· is of such importance to instil early into the minds of young men who are to make their own way in the world.

As these characteristics, indeed, pervade the whole book, I confidently trust it may gain favour with the public, and lead to others no less instructive and amusing to young readers.

I remain

Your most obedient

Humble Servant,

BASIL HALL.

Edinburgh, 11th Oct. 1837.